PENGUIN BOOKS

# WHERE HAVE ALL THE BULLETS GONE?

Spike Milligan was one of the greatest and most influential comedians of the twentieth century. Born in India in 1918, he was educated in India and England before joining the Royal Artillery at the start of the Second World War and serving in North Africa and Italy. At the end of the war, he forged a career as a jazz musician, sketch-show writer and performer, touring Europe with the Bill Hall Trio and the Ann Lenner Trio, before joining forces with, among others, Peter Sellers and Harry Secombe, to create the legendary *Goon Show*. Broadcast on BBC Radio, the ten series of the *Goon Show* ran from 1951 until 1960 and brought Spike to international fame, as well as to the edge of sanity and the break-up of his first marriage. He had subsequent success as a stage and film actor, as the author of over eighty books of fiction, memoir, poetry, plays, cartoons and children's stories, and with his long-running one-man show. In 1992 he was made a CBE and in 2001 an honorary KBE, and in 2000 and 2001 he received two Lifetime Achievement Awards for writing and for comedy. He died in 2002.

SPIKE MILLIGAN

# Where Have
# All the Bullets Gone?

PENGUIN BOOKS

PENGUIN BOOKS

Published by the Penguin Group
Penguin Books Ltd, 80 Strand, London WC2R 0RL, England
Penguin Group (USA) Inc., 375 Hudson Street, New York, New York 10014, USA
Penguin Group (Canada), 90 Eglinton Avenue East, Suite 700, Toronto, Ontario, Canada M4P 2Y3
(a division of Pearson Penguin Canada Inc.)
Penguin Ireland, 25 St Stephen's Green, Dublin 2, Ireland (a division of Penguin Books Ltd)
Penguin Group (Australia), 250 Camberwell Road, Camberwell, Victoria 3124, Australia
(a division of Pearson Australia Group Pty Ltd)
Penguin Books India Pvt Ltd, 11 Community Centre, Panchsheel Park, New Delhi – 110 017, India
Penguin Group (NZ), 67 Apollo Drive, Rosedale, Auckland 0632, New Zealand
(a division of Pearson New Zealand Ltd)
Penguin Books (South Africa) (Pty) Ltd, Block D, Rosebank Office Park,
181 Jan Smuts Avenue, Parktown North, Gauteng 2193, South Africa

Penguin Books Ltd, Registered Offices: 80 Strand, London WC2R 0RL, England

www.penguin.com

First published by M & J Hobbs and Michael Joseph 1985
Published in Penguin Books 1986
Reissued in this edition 2012
This edition published 2012 for The Book People Ltd,
Hall Wood Avenue, Haydock, St Helens, WA11 9UL

001

Printed in England by Clays Ltd, St Ives plc

ISBN: 978-0-241-96449-1

www.greenpenguin.co.uk

ALWAYS LEARNING                    **PEARSON**

To my wife Sheila

In my previous war books, alas, to my sorrow, some of those mentioned took offence at some of the references, which of course were intended to be humorous. But then you can't please everybody, as the late Adolf Hitler said, so in this book I have used fictitious names. I would still like to add that the book is intended to be humorous.

*Spike Milligan*

# Foreword

The title of this book is a phrase remembered down the years. As I was lying on a makeshift bed in a rain-ridden tent alongside a Scots Guardsman, Jock Rogers, in a camp for the bomb-happy miles behind the firing line, I realized that for the first time in a year and a half, I was not worrying about mortar bombs, shells or Spandaus, and I said to him 'Where have all the bullets gone?' I had totally forgotten this utterance until one night, during a visit to South Africa, I was arriving at the theatre and there outside the stage door was the tall lean Scots Guardsman, now grey but still as positive as ever. 'Where have all the bullets gone?' he said. A quick drink and we were back to those haunting days in Italy in 1944, at the foot of Mount Vesuvius, with lava running in great red rivulets down the slope towards *us*, and Jock taking a drag on his cigarette and saying, 'I think we've got grounds for a rent rebate.' He was one of many who entered and left my life in the years 1944 and '45, and in this book I have begun the story with my leaving the front line Regiment (19 Battery 56 Heavy Field RA) and frigging around in a sort of khaki limbo until someone found a job for me to do. It was all to lead to my making the world of entertainment my profession, but when you think that you have to have a world war to find the right job, it makes you think. Here it is then.

Foxcombe House,                                          Spike Milligan
South Harting,
Hampshire.
January 1985

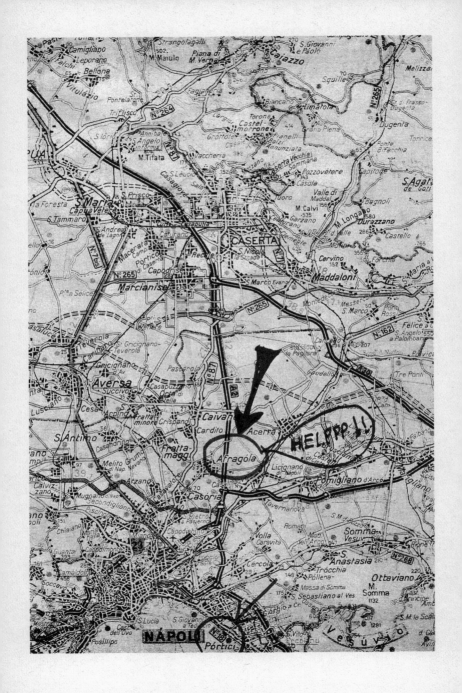

# AFRAGOLA

# Afragola

What *is* an Afragola? An Afragola is a small grotty suburb of Bella Napoli. Named after a Centurion who performed a heroic deed against Spartacus and Co: he hit one of them and in return was killed. A grateful Emperor named this spot in his honour. It was a spot I wouldn't give to a leopard. A field adjacent to this 'spot' is now a transit camp for 'bomb-happy' soldiers and *I* was now 'bomb-happy', having been dumped here, along with some untreated sewage, following treatment at No. 2 General Hospital, Caserta. After several medical boards, I was down-graded to B2, considered loony and 'unfit to be killed in combat' by either side. My parents were so disappointed.

It's a bleak misty day with new added drizzle for extra torment. Mud! How did it climb up your body, over your hat, and back down into your boots? The camp's official title is REHABILITATION. *Oxford Dictionary*: Rehabilitation: Dealing with the restoration of the maimed and unfit to a place in society. So! *Now* I was maimed, unfit, and about to be restored to a place in society! The camp was a mixture of 'loonies' and 'normals'. One couldn't tell the difference, save during air-raids when the loonies dropped everything and ran screaming in the direction of away, crying 'Mummy'. Today mud and men were standing around in huddled groups or sitting in the tents with the flaps up; our camp emblem should have been a dead hippopotamus. A Sergeant Arnolds appears to be 'running the camp' . . . into the ground. He was to organization what Arthur Scargill was to landscape gardening. Would I like to be a unit clerk? Why? He had spotted a pencil in my pocket. The job has advantages – excused parades for one, and I sleep in a large marquee, which is the office. Having a tilly lamp put me in the 'that rotten bastard can read in bed' category.

At ten of a morning, a lorry would arrive bearing the latest intake of 'loonies'. I would document them on large foolscap forms that were never asked for, nor ever seen again. The weather is foul, or more, duck. The damp!

Matches, like Tories, wouldn't strike, fags went out and never came back, paper wouldn't crackle, blankets had the sickly sweet smell of death. Men took their battledresses to bed to keep them dry and, sometimes, for companionship.

## February 14

ST VALENTINE'S DAY AND BRONCHITIS

From the pelting rain a lone guardsman reports to the tent, wrung out – he could become a tributary of the Thames. He's got fish in his pockets and is going mouldy. Tall, thin, a dark Celtic image, a Scots Guard, though covered in so much muck he could well be a Mud Guard. He dumps his kit in the marquee. It goes Squeegeee! Sergeant Arnolds cautions him: 'Yew, kinnot sleep hin 'ere.' The guardsman's face screws up: 'I'm fuckin' stayin' in here Jamie, and no cunt is gonna ha me oot.' Arnolds exits muttering threats. Guardsman 'Jock' Rogers becomes resident and, to save face, Sergeant Arnolds appoints him 'Runner', even though he only walks.

Helping lose the war is the army food. Cordon Brown. Bully beef! The meat in these tins was from beasts, proud descendants of cattle introduced by the Conquistadores of Cortez to graze and grow fat on the lush sunlit pastures of the Aztecs. Now lukewarm bits of them were floating around my mess tin, in watery gravy. 'I've seen cows hurt worse than this and live,' says Guardsman Rogers. I had never seen trasparent custard before. Rogers is convinced that the cooks will be tried as war criminals. A camel couldn't pass through the eye of a needle, he says, but his breakfast could.

'Hello, Milligan.'

I look up from my forms. It's my old D Battery Skipper, Captain Martin.

'What are you doing here?'

I say I'm doing my best. He shoots a glance at my sleeve. 'My stripes are at the cleaners, sir, getting the blood off.' I tell him I'm here because I'm a 'loony'. He departs for the UK.

I never saw him again. I wonder if he survived. He never attended Battery reunions. Perhaps he was killed, which is one way of avoiding Battery reunions.

## News

Fighting on the Cassino front is savage, like World War I. My God! They've bombed the Monastery into rubble. I can't believe it. It's true. We must be bloody mad ... I know the head Abbot was, oh the bill for repairs ...

New intakes are arriving. All ask that haunting question. 'What's going to happen to me?' I try and reassure them. 'You'll be OK here, chum.' I wished I could have said: 'I see a dark millionairess who will soothe the swelling and lay hands on you.'

Hope is coming! An ENSA Concert Party! Strong men broke down and cried, others knelt and prayed, the rest faced England and sang 'Jerusalem'. Would it be sing-you-to-death Gracie Fields? Michael Wilding and his wig? In anticipation we all waited in a muddy field for its arrival. It appeared in the form of a large American lorry which backed towards us. On the tailboard a sign: ENSA PRESENTS THE TAILBOARD FOLLIES. The tailboard is lowered by a dwarf-like driver (cheers). The back flaps still hanging, the bottom half of a piano and a pianist are revealed, also the bottom half of a man in evening dress who throws up the flaps (cheers). He is a middle-aged man who has been dead ten years. He wrestles a microphone down to his height. 'Last man was taller than me,' he says in the embarrassed tones of a comic who will never make it. 'Well,' he chortled, 'here we are.' Bloody fool, we all knew where we were. 'First, to cheer you up, is our pianist Doris Terrible!' (Cheers). This is the old dear whose top half now reveals that she's about sixty-five, and also dead. Heavily rouged and mascaraed, a masterpiece of the embalmer's art, she plunged into the piano as if it were a wash tub. 'Ma, he's making eyes at me', 'Blue Birds over the White Cliffs of Dover'. On she thundered, the lorry shaking under the assault. We give her an ovation. 'Now boys,' she yodelled, 'what would you like to hear next?' A Cockney voice: 'We'd like to hear some bloody music.' She pretends to laugh, but we notice her hands are clenching and unclenching like the Boston Strangler's, whom she later became. Again the mike-wrestling compère. He tells a few crappy gags. I suppose he meant well, but then so did Hitler. Ah, this is better! The Rumpo Twins! Two blondes, dressed as sailors with short skirts, tap dance and sing through 'The Fleet's in Port Again'. Big cheers, whistles, and 'Get 'em down.'

'Here to sing melodies divine is Gravard Lax.' A time-ravaged middle-aged very fat tenor comes forward. 'Lend us yer ration book,' comes a cry.

'Good evening,' he says in a high catarrhal voice, like snails had crawled up his nose. 'Itt-isser, a greattt pleasurer-errr, to beee-er here-er to-nighttt-er.'

'You're lucky to be anywhere tonight.' A voice.

'Ha ha ha-er' says the singer, meaning 'You Bastard-er.' 'I would like to sing the Bowmen of England-er.'

'Then why don't you?'

Mrs Terrible thunders the intro. Now, it so happens, at that very moment, a squadron of Heinkel bombers, with the engines cut, were gliding in to bomb Naples and/or Mrs Terrible and her piano. The engines roar into life, followed by the ascending banshee wail of the sirens, which synchronize with the opening of the tenor's mouth. 'My God,' said Guardsman Rogers, 'he's singing the air-raid warning.' Bombs start to drop, the entire audience vanishes and the driver slips the lorry into gear and drives away. I watched transfixed with laughter as the tenor, still singing 'The Bowmen' was transported to safety, staggering and holding the sides of the lorry as they turned left and drove up the road to Afragola. He was still in full song as he disappeared into the darkness and I could only wonder when he stopped

# $\mathfrak{H}$itlergram $\mathfrak{No}.\mathfrak{Eins}$

**HITLER:** Hello Goering? How did zer air-raid go?

**GOERING:** Ve are breaking up zer Tailboard Follies, for zem zer war is over. Next time, Tommy Trinder, Ann Shelton and Micheal Wilding and his wig!

**HITLER:** Gut. Soon Vera Lynn and zer White Cliffs of Dover Sole will sue for peace.

– did he reach Cassino? They don't write songs like that any more.


**February 30**

The day after, a notice appears on Part Two orders: 'The ENSA Concert is cancelled until further notice.' The war seems to have stopped, the weather and casualties have ground our advance to a halt. If no news is good news, we must all be delirious with happiness. Guardsman Rogers has been posting little pieces of mud home. 'Dear Mother, This is a piece of mud. When you have enough, stand on it, and have a holiday in sunny Italy.' The days pass, life is like a clock with no hands. – Wait! Excitement beckons. An Inspection? INSPECTION???? HERE??? Everybody's covered in mud! We're ankle deep in it! We are all shit order! Yet, somewhere the British Army have found a Colonel suffering from I-must-have-an-inspection withdrawal symptoms. A BBC documentary of what followed, would go thus:

COMM: Well here we are on the great field of mud inspection parade (sound of rain, thunder and groans). Some ten thousand tons of mud have been flown in especially to simulate the Somme. The troops are wearing their best battledress with their best mud on it. It's a proud sight as the Colonel walks along the ranks of slowly sinking men. He's stopped to talk to a soldier in a hole. But it's too late, he's drowned.

It was a proud day for the British Army and a hysterical one for me. If only Hitler had known.

## Hitlergram No. Zwei

HITLER: If only I had known.
GOEBBELS: If only you had known vat?
HITLER: *That's* vat I don't know.

Mud and trench foot have triumphed! We move to 92 General Naples! Here we are in warm dry billets and for a time the administration was taken over by the hospital, so Jock and I were 'spare wanks' but were told to 'Stand by'. We did. We 'stood by'. What we were standing by for we knew not, but whenever we were asked. 'What are you men doing?' we replied 'Standing by, sir' and it sufficed.

Naples, land of Wine, Women and Syph. The Borsa Nera! My parents sent me all my post office savings – no good leaving it mouldering in England when here I could become rich, rich, rich! In time it arrived, smuggled in a box cunningly marked Pile Suppositories. My parents were no fools. Six pounds! Wait till this money hits the black market! Next evening, on the Via Roma, I made contact.

'Hey, Joe,' (he'd got my name wrong!) 'you wanna change money or a fuck?'

'Sterling,' I said out of the corner of my mouth.

'How mucha you gotta?'

I smiled secretively. I handed him the Pile Suppository box.

He shook out the money. 'Six pounds?' he said. 'Is datta all?' He was joking, he was just trying to play it cool.

I nodded like James Cagney and I made with the shoulders. 'What's the rate?' I said, this time as George Raft. Two thousand lire. Great. The hit man looked up and down the street. 'You waita here, wid my two a friends.' He indicated two young urchins and made off.

'He go makea da deal,' said the eldest.

I waited. We all waited. 'He takea longa time,' said one urchin. 'I go see whata happen' and left. Three down, one to go. We wait.

'Something ees a wrong, I go and see, you waita herea.'

And none to go. I waited 'herea', the evening dew settled on me, midnight, I waited 'herea' for three hours. Technically I'm still waiting. James Cagney, George Raft and Bombardier Milligan have been conned. I walked back down the Via Roma as Charlie Chaplin.

'Wanna buy cigarette Americano?' A young urchin hove to.

Yes! I'll get my own back! I'll buy cigarettes cheap! Twenty Philip Morris. It was strange – the ship bearing my six pounds in a Pile Suppository box had risked U-boats, dive bombers, all that bravery for nothing.

Back at the 92 General, Rogers is waiting expectantly. 'Well, ha' you got spondulicks?' he said, rubbing his hands. I tell my woeful story, he laughs at each revelation. Never mind, have a real American cigarette. I open a packet like John Wayne, give the base a flick, sawdust spurts out. Rogers laughs out loud. Sawdust! 'Why not start a circus?' he says, ducking a boot at his head.

# TORRE DEL GRECO

## Torre Del Greco

Torre Del Greco was a dust and rags village astride the Salerno-Naples Road on the south side of Vesuvius. It was adjacent to this that a new tented camp had been erected for our 'loonies'. A short journey by lorry saw us settling in. It was life as per Afragola. The warm weather had come and we watched as the sun dried out our mud-caked men, making them look like fossilized corpses of Turkish Janissaries. The office tent is in among olive groves, yes. Olive Groves, the diva that sang with Ivor Novello. Who could christen a child Olive Groves? Why not Walnut Trees?

A letter from my mother gives dire warning of the coming shortage of underwear in England. 'You would be wise to stock up now, son,' she urges. 'It's already started. Neighbours have stopped hanging their laundry out and your father sleeps with his underwear on for safety.' Obeying my mother's warning, I bought, stole, cajoled a mass of underwear, from a series of holes on a waist band to heavily patched beer-stained transparent long-johns.

From the medical board I had received my 'U are now officially down-graded' papers. I was still glad to see on the certificate that I had Hernia . . . Nil, Varicose Veins . . . Nil, a draw! I also noted that I had No Gynaecological disorders. I wrote and told my mother I was B2. She wrote back: 'Your father and I are so proud, none of our family have ever had the B2 before.'

## March 1944

It was spring, the sun shone and the mud disappeared. Banging his boot on the ground, Guardsman Rogers exclaims: 'My God! I think I've found land!'

## The New Broom Cweeps Slean

The camp is to be run by a loony officer; he's been blown up on the Volturno and blown down again at Cassino. Captain

Peters of the Queens. Tall and thin, large horse-like face, pale blue eyes with a rapid blink and a twitch of the head; all done with a strange noise at the back of the nose that goes 'phnut'. He is balding and has a fine head of hairs. Speaks very rapidly due to an overdraft at Lloyds.

To date one had the feeling that the Rehabilitation Camp was totally unknown and unrecorded in the Army lists. With the coming of Captain Peters all that changed. The camp went on being unknown and unrecorded, but now we had an officer in charge. The camp had a turnover of about a thousand men, all in a state of coming and going, unlike me who couldn't tell if I was coming or going. Under Peters the food improved. He indented for twice the amount, and sent scrounging parties to buy eggs, chicken and fish, all of which the cooks dutifully boiled to shreds. 'I think they put it in with the laundry,' said Peters. He also allowed men out of an evening, but the effect of alcohol on some of the loonies who were on tranquillizers was alarming. It was something to see the guard commander and his men holding down a half naked shit-covered, wine-stained loony alternately being sick, screaming and singing. Some loonies tried to climb Vesuvius. God knows how many fell in. A resident psychiatrist arrived. He immediately dished out drugs that zombified most of the inmates, who walked around the camp staring-eyed, grinning and saying 'Hello' to trees.

## March 5

DIARY: HIGH TEMPERATURE REPORTED SICK

'You've got Gingivitis,' said the M.O.

'Gingivitis?'

'It's inflamed gums.' I see. A sort of Trench Foot of the mouth.

'It was very common in World War One.'

'Is it a better class now?'

'Do you clean your teeth regularly?'

'Yes, once a week.'

'You've got it quite badly, you can pick it up anywhere.'
'Not in the legs surely?'
He smiled. 'I'm putting you in the 70th General.'
The 70th! I'd done the 92nd, now the 70th! BINGO! 'Gunner Milligan, you have just won the golden thermometer!'

## 70th General Hospital Pompeii

A long cool ward full of military illnesses. Through the window I see a wall with faded Fascist slogans: OBBIDIRE, CREDERE, LAVORARE, MUSSOLINI HA SEMPRE RAGGIONE. Obey, believe, work. Three words that would send a British Leyland worker into a swoon.

A gay nurse leads me to my bed. 'Put those on.' He points to some blue pyjamas. Each side of me are two soldiers with bronchitis. They are asleep. When they wake up they still have it. One is from Lewisham, the other isn't. The gay nurse returns and takes my temperature.

'What is it?'

'It's a thermometer,' he says and minces off.

A doctor appears escorted by a Matron with a huge bosom. She tapers away and disappears at the waist. She has Eton-cropped hair and a horsy face and if you shouted 'Gee up', she would gallop away. They stop at bed-ends to check patients' records. Who will be in the top ten? Last week it was Corporal Welts with Ulcerated Groin, but coming up from nowhere and coming in at Number two is Gunner Milligan and Real Disease with Gingivitis! My God, it's the drunken sandy-haired Scots doctor from Volume II! How did he find his way into Volume V? 'See,' he mused, 'I know yew, see, Salerno wasn't it?'

'Yes sir, last time I had Salerno.' Matron hands him my chart which is lost from sight as she heaves it from under her bosom.

The gay nurse arrives. 'I've got to paint your gums.'

'I want someone better than you – Augustus John, Renoir . . .'

He applies the scalding Gentian Violet. It tastes like cats' piss boiled in turpentine. A brilliant purple colour.

The days pass. A parcel delivery. By the shape it must have been a Caesarian. Now the hot weather has arrived, my mother has sent me a balaclava and gloves, plus three socks. She explains: 'One is a spare, son.' I lay them on my bed to rest.

'There's one short,' says Lewisham.

'No, no, they're all the same length,' I say.

'I mean, shouldn't there be four?' says Lewisham.

'No, my mother always makes three, you see, I have a one-legged brother.'

Lewisham goes mute, but he has his uses: he has a bird who visits him with a pretty sister who is soon onto me. I hide my three socks in case she thinks I've got three legs, or two legs and a willy warmer. She is short plump and pretty. Her name is Maria. (All girls in Italy not called Mussolini are called Maria.) Tea and biscuits are being served. We sit and talk broken Italian and biscuits. In the days that follow she brings me grapes, figs, oranges and apples. I get clinical dysentery.

## March 10

DIARY: CURED!

I can leave today. A tearful farewell with Maria. She loads me with another bag of diaretics. 'Come back soon,' she says.

An ambulance drops me off at my little grey home in the marquee where Guardsman Rogers is waiting. 'Thank God you're back,' he says. I promise as soon as I see him I will. He's been snowed under with office work, he's been working his head to the bone, etc., etc. All this was to pale into insignificance at what was to come.

# Volcanoes, Their Uses in World War II

Yes, Vesuvius had started to belch smoke at an alarming rate, and at night tipples of lava were spilling over the cone. Earth tremors were felt; there was no more inadequate place for a thousand bomb-happy loonies. An area order: 'People at the base of the Volcano should be advised to leave.' Signed Town Major, Portici, a hundred miles away. Captain Peters is telling me that as I speak the 'Iti' to 'take the jeep and tell those people,' he waves a walking stick out to sea, 'tell them it's dangerous for them to stay!' Bloody fool, it was like telling Sir Edmund Hillary: 'I must warn you that Mount Everest is the highest mountain in the world.'

It was evening when I set out in the jeep. Due to the smoke, it was dark before sunset. A strange unearthly light settled on the land, reminding me of those Turner chiaroscuro paintings. Up the little winding roads through fields of dark volcanic soil. I did it, but I felt bloody silly shouting out 'Attenzione! E pericoloso rimanere qui!'

I stopped at the last farm up the slopes. It was dark now, the mountain rumbling and the cone glowing scarlet like the throat of a mythical dragon. A yellow glow in a window. A little short weathered farmer is standing at the door. At my approach he waves. I give him the message. He appears to have got it already: 'Vesuvio, molto cattivo.'

'Si,' I said. I was fluent in 'sis.'

Would I like some wine?

'Si.'

He beckons me into his home. Accustomed to the gloom, I see a humble adobe room. An oil lamp shows simple things, a table, chairs, a sideboard with yellowing photos; a candle burns before the Virgin, possibly the only one in the area. In the centre of the room is a large circular stone, hollowed out and burning charcoal. Around it sit the farmer's twin daughters.

As I entered, they stood up, smiling; identical twins, about five foot four, wearing knee-length rough black woollen dresses, black woollen stockings to the knee and wooden-sole sandals. Madre? 'Madre morta. Tedesco fusillato.' Killed by a stray shell which he blamed on the Germans. The girls were fourteen, making a total of twenty-eight.

We sat and drank red wine. Motherless at fourteen, a war on, and the mountain about to blow. It was worse than Catford. The girls sat close together, heads inclined towards each other, they radiated sweetness and innocence.

The farmer is weatherbeaten. If not the weather, then *someone* has beaten the shit out of him; he has hands like ploughed fields. He is telling me his family have been here since – he makes a gesture, it's timeless. I could be talking to the head gardener from the House of Pansa at the time of Nero. His trousers certainly are.

I drove back by the light of Vesuvius, it saved the car batteries. The lava was now flowing down the sides towards the sea, the rumbling was very loud. The camp was all awake and in a state of tension. Men stood outside their tents staring at the phenomenon, their faces going on and off in the volcano's fluctuating light. It was all very exciting, you didn't get this sort of stuff in Brockley SE26.

The volcano claimed its first victim. A forty-year-old Private from the Pioneer Corps dies from a heart attack. Captain Peters was not a man to worry about such things. 'He'll miss the eruption,' he said, under great pressure trying to calm the camp of loonies. 'Keep calm,' he shouted to himself, popping pills all the while. Men were running away from the camp. It presented a problem.

---

REX vs VOLCANOES

COLONEL: What is the charge?
CAPT. P: Desertion in the face of volcanoes.
COLONEL: Has he deserted his volcanoes before?
CAPT. P: No, sir, his volcano record is spotless.

---

Earth tremors are coming up the legs and annoying the groins but nothing falls off. Naples is in a state of high anxiety; church bells ringing, Ities praying, dogs barking, alarmed birds chirping flitting from tree to tree; some of the camp loonies are also chirping and flitting from tree to tree.

## Diary: March 21

Very dark morning, heavy rumblings. Is it Vesuvius? No, it's Jock. It was my day off. I hitched a ride to Naples and the Garrison Theatre to see Gracie Fields in 'Sing As We Go'. Having never sung as I'd been, I was keen to see how it was done. It was terrible, so terrible that I thought that at any moment she would sing the bloody awful Warsaw Concerto. She was on to her hundredth 'Eee bai gum' when the shit hit the fan. The whole theatre shook, accompanied by labyrinthine rumblings. Vesuvius had blown its top. The

audience became a porridge of screams and shouts of 'What the fuck was that?' all the while hurtling towards the exit. It coincided with Gracie Fields, followed by spanner-clutching extras, marching towards the screen singing 'Sing As We Go'. It looked as if the screaming mass were trying to escape from her. I alone was in hysterics. Outside was no laughing matter – the sky was black with ash, and Vesuvius roaring like a giant monster.

Rivulets of lava, like burst veins, were rolling down the seaward side. The streets were full of people walking fast with the shits.

I thumbed a lift. 'Torre Del Greco?'

'You must be bleedin' mad,' said a driver.

I assured him I was.

'That's where all the bloody lava's going.'

'Yes,' I said, 'lava come back to me.' Not much of a joke in 1985, but at the time I was an amateur soldier, not a professional comic, and it wasn't a bad joke for an earth-quake.

No lifts, so I walk; it starts to rain a mixture of ash and water, bringing with it lumps of pumice the size of marbles. So this is what Dystopia was like. I trudge wearily down the road to Pompeii. But wait! This was the very road trod by Augustus, Nero, Tiberius, even the great Julius Caesar, and I thought 'Fuck 'em' and was well pleased. All the while people are running in and out of their homes like those Swiss weather clocks.

A black American driver pulls up: 'Wanna lift?'

I don't need a lift, I need a lorry and he has one. Yes, he's going to 'Torrey Del Greckoe'. He offers me a cigarette, then gum, then chocolate. I wait for money but nothing comes. The fall of ash has turned his hair grey. He looked every bit like Uncle Tom. I stopped short of asking how little Eva was, or how big Eva was now. When we arrived at the Loony Camp it was pitch-black and so was he. 'Goodbye,' said his teeth.

The camp was in a state of 'chassis'. Half the loonies had bolted, and the Ities were looting the camp. Captain Peters has organized the sane, issued them with pickaxe handles, and they were somewhere up the slopes belting the life out of thieving Ities. The guard were alerted and roaming the perimeter with loaded rifles.

'Captain Peters told us to shoot on sight,' they said.

'Shoot what on sight?' I said.

'Oh, he didn't go into details,' they said.

There was nothing for it but to lie back and enjoy it. What am I waiting for? – there is the jeep unoccupied. I put it in gear and drive off, headlights full on to penetrate the viscous gloom. I stop to purchase two bottles of Lachryma Christi, and on to the gates of Pompeii Veccia, La Scavi! A short walk to the Porta Marina, down the Via Marina, the Via Abbondanza, then square on in the Strada Stabiana and there at the end pulsates Vesuvius! I swig the wine. It's all heady stuff. I'm in a time warp, this is A D 79. The streets are rippling with fleeing Pompeiians, except, I recall, the plaster cast of the couple screwing. What courage, banging away with red hot cinders bouncing off your bum. What courage, the first case of someone coming and going at the same time. The roar of the mountain is blanketing the countryside. More wine. I make my way to the house of Meander, the wall frescos dancing in the fibrillating light, Fauns, Nymphs, more wine, Leda, Bacchus, more wine, Ariadne, Lily Dunford, Betty Grable, someone with big boobs. I finish the wine and it finished me. What a night! For three hours I had been Pliny. I had also been pissed.

I drove back to the camp in great humour. The camp guard is Polish. He gets it all wrong. 'Health my friend! What goes on there?'

'The green swan of the East meets the grey bear,' I said.

'Pass it up,' he said.

I'm told that Captain Peters has gone to the Portici to 'An Officers' Dance'. 'What is it?' I said. 'Firewalking?'

I fell asleep knowing I'd never have another day like that.

I was wrong. I awoke and it *was* another day just like that. The cooks had 'buggered off'. We raided the cookhouse and made breakfast, porridge and volcanic ash. The grey

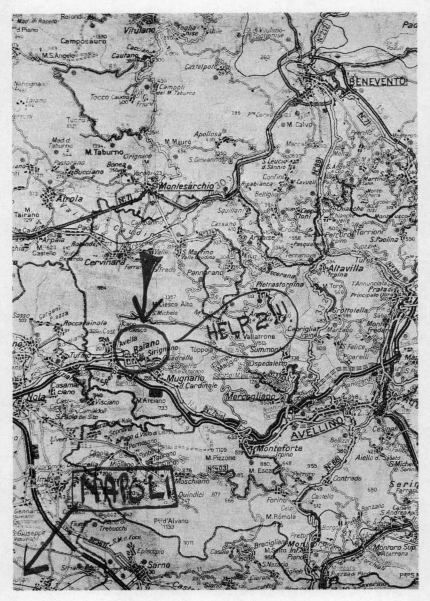

*Map showing Baiano*

powdery fall-out was everywhere. It looked like a plague of dandruff.

Captain Peters approaches, waving his stick and cracking his shin in the process. 'Ah! Milligan, I'm putting you and phnut! Rogers in charge.' Why? There isn't anybody else. 'I'm off to the Town Major's. If any of the cooks come back, phnut! put them under arrest.'

'Is that for cooking or deserting?'

The eruption reached its zenith that day, and then all was quiet; but the breakdown of all organization at the camp must have reached the ear of someone who decided that loonies need peace and tranquillity to recover, and so it came to pass.

'We are moving to a place called Baiano.' The Guardsman has spoken. The farming village of Baiano lay N E of Naples, by about twenty kilometres, on a bad day thirty (see map).

'I will, phnut, drive,' said Captain Peters, talking to the steering wheel of the jeep. A dry sunny day, the Captain dons dust goggles, thinks he's Biggles. 'Hold tight,' he shouts, and with the engine roaring, engages every gear and stalls. We lurch away, our bodies rocketing back and forth like hiccuping drunks. Simple single-storey buildings line our route, in clusters, then occasional spaces like missing teeth. Now and then an affluent neo-classical villa. Dust has us putting handkerchiefs round our faces; we look like an armed posse after Billy the Kid. Midday, we reach Nola, a dusty working/middle-class city.

'We'll stop here for phnut! refreshments,' says the Captain, pulling up outside a trattoria. We sit at an outside table, sipping coffee and brandy. The lass who served us, Oh! help me! she's lush, dark, boobs, buttocks, a smile like a piano keyboard, eyes like Bambi, and oh! those dimples on the back of her knees. A line of Shermans on tank transporters rumble and clank through the Piazza. There was still a war on.

'I suppose some of those will become coffins for some poor bastards,' says Sergeant Arnolds, himself an ex-tank man.

Having unwound his neck from staring at the waitress, Captain Peters says 'This used to be a phnut! Roman garrison town.' This remark brought forth absolutely no response, in fact the silence became positively an embarrassment. I tried to help.

'That was very nice of you to tell us that this was a Roman garrison town.'

'Oh,' he said, smilingly, 'think nothing of it.' In fact we didn't think anything of it.

The bill. Captain Peters carries out a vigorous patting of his pockets, the best display of overacting I've ever seen. 'Damn,' he says, 'I've come out without any money.' He was a known mean bastard. On pay day, before his money even saw the light of day, it was into an envelope on its way 'To the little woman who needs it'. He would have had us believe it was an impoverished female dwarf.

Revenge is sweet, but not fattening. After the war I was about to open an account at Lloyds of Lewisham and I was to meet the manager. My God, it was Captain Peters. 'Milligan,' he said joyfully.

Hurriedly I started patting my pockets. 'Damn,' I said, 'I've come out without any money, the little woman needs it.' To my lasting joy I still have an unpaid overdraft there – ten shillings since 1949.

Early afternoon, and we arrived at the little village of Baiano with its paved grid-orientated streets lined with two-storeyed buildings. The affluent lived in the outskirts in cool villas. Set in flat farming country with a range of low hills running east-west along the north side. The main street had shops cheek by jowl with goods on show outside – sacks of lentils, grain, beans, flour. The butcher displayed miserable bits of meat, but fish was plentiful – squid, octopus, prawns, mussels – and occasionally the monger throws a bucket of water to freshen them up and drown the flies. There's an old-fashioned pharmacy with large glass jars of red and green water; more anon.

# BAIANO

## The Baiano Rehabilitation Camp

The camp is half a mile outside the town adjacent to a cemetery. The entrance is flanked by two Nissen huts, one the general office, the other the Captain's office. A white-washed logo of stones spells out REINFORCEMENT RE-ALLOCATION AND TRAINING CENTRE. It's laid out on a tented grid system and the camp centre has a large dining tent. Across the road in a light green villa is the new 'Officers' Wing', made necessary by the increasing number of bomb-happy officers. 'It would be demoralizing, phnut, for the officers to be bomb-happy in front of the phnut! ORs,' says Peters, who is bomb-happy in front of us all the time.

The setting was very tranquil, away from noise, war and volcanoes. 'You see,' said my Scots prophet, Rogers, 'we'll never be bloody heard of again.'

---

WHITEHALL 1952

*The Scene:* CHURCHILL lays on a couch being massaged with brandy by a GENERAL.

ALANBROOKE: Isn't it time we brought them home?

CHURCHILL: No, they're loonies – they'll vote Labour.

ALANBROOKE: We've had letters from Milligan's mother and father.

CHURCHILL: It's more than he has.

ALANBROOKE: They want to thank you for keeping him out there, and to announce a room to let with gas ring and kipper fork, twelve shillings per week.

CHURCHILL: Tell General de Gaulle we've found him an embassy.

---

## Orginisateum

A complete office and service staff have arrived, including Private Dick Shepherd, a medical orderly from Rochdale. His knowledge of medicine goes like this: 'Soldiers laying down are sick ones.' A clerk in the form of Private 'Bronx' Weddon of the Berkshires, both misnomers – he had been neither to the Bronx nor Berkshire. He was from Brighton, but you couldn't go around saying: 'I'm Brighton Weddon.' He said he was 'A journalist who worked for Marley Tiles'. I didn't get the drift. Another addition was the Camp 'Runner', Private Andrews; that is, at the mention of work he started to run. He had an accent like three Billy Connollys, he hated the army, he hated the job, he hated the world and all the planets adjacent.

'Luk herrre, Spike, no fuckerrr everrr got anywherrrre being a fucking runerrrr.'

How wrong he was, what about Jesse Owens, Sidney Wooderson?

'Who the fuck are they mon?'

He wasn't that thick. A heavy smoker, well on his way to lung cancer, he was forever on the earole for fags and, here's the cunning of the man, if you didn't give him one he would stand beside you and howl like a wolf. In any well-ordered society he would have been taken away, but in this camp he was considered normal. He could be pinpointed, suddenly, as from some distant tent came unearthly howling.

Captain Peters once asked: 'What is that?'

I told him, 'Private Andrews.'

'Oh, he's phnut! very good at it,' said Peters, who wasn't too bad at it himself.

We now have a 15cwt truck and driver. He is private Jim Brockenbrow. His father had been a POW in World War I, stayed in England and married a lass from Mousehole. The fruit of that union, now known as that 'square-headed bastard', he would defend his Teutonic ancestry with a Cornish accent.

'Luk'ere, them Germans hain't bad fellas, it's them bluddy Narzees that's the narsty buggerrrss.'

Andrews will have none of it. 'Listen Jamie, the fuckin' Germans are fitin' on the same side as the fuckin' Nazis.'

'Oo arr, but them's not memburs o' the Narzee party.'

'Awa fuckin' hame, there's nay fuckin' difference, they all shute tae kill, that's why I'm fuckin' herrrre.'

He had a point. Poor Brockenbrow, they ragged him stupid. ''ere 'itler, take this package to Town Major Portici, don't give it to Goebbels on the way.'

FRED SHEPHERD

JOCK ROGERS

*Photo of office personnel*
*\* this man is now in South Africa somewhere*

37

## Daily Life in the Camp

Reveille at 0700, Roll call at 0730, Breakfast at 0800. Parade 0915. Sick Parade and Defaulters 1000. Everything was organized. We had typewriters, filing cabinets, inter-camp phones, electric light, but no mangle.

I was having recurring bouts of depression, just suddenly black, black gloom. I was missing the Battery. I wrote what must have been an embarrassing letter to the C.O. Major Jenkins. It was snivelling and grovelling, asking to be forgiven for failing in the action at Colle Dimiano; would he give me another chance, anything, I'd do anything to come back. I'd go insane if I stayed here. It demanded a reply if only on humanitarian grounds. He never replied. He was an officer and a gentleman, so fuck him, but, he was a good soldier and a pain in the arse . . . all over.

It's a nice morning. I'm in the office sipping tea I've brought from breakfast. A new intake arrives, a big batch, over a hundred. Bronx and I are documenting them. 'Next, please,' I say in my cheer-up-chum voice, and there was Lance Bombardier Reg Bennett from our North Africa concert party. He bursts into tears. 'Don't cry, Reg, there's a drought on.' An attempt to joke him out of it. He's from the 74 Mediums, a sister regiment. The Americans had bombed his position on the terrible day of the Monastery disaster. 'We were bloody miles away, but bloody miles from the Monastery. Why me? Do I look like a Monastery?' His friends had been killed and wounded, and it had done for him.

Now he disagrees with my version of our meeting. He says: *'I came to the camp and you weren't in the office when I came through. I was in the camp two days, and I was going out of my mind with depression and boredom when one day I heard the sound of a trumpet coming from a tent. I thought, Christ, it's Spike. I came over, threw back the tent flap and there you were laying on the bed blowing your bugle. I remember putting my mess tins full of dinner down to shake hands with you.'*

If, after forty years, our stories differ so much, how many

changes has the Bible gone through? Did Jesus meet Paul on the road to Damascus or was it Lance Bombardier Bennett? 'I thought I heard you playing the trumpet, Jesus.' 'No,' says Jesus, 'that was Milligan. You haven't seen Bombardier Bennett, around, have you?'

Reg was in a bad way, tense and lachrymose. I took him down town in the evening and we sat in a Vino Bar drinking white wine. Of an evening, the people of Baiano emptied out on to the streets and sat in little groups at their doors, mothers, fathers, children, uncles, aunts, all chatting away, laughing or lamenting the state of the world. Like we watch 'Dallas', the Italians watched German air-raids over Naples, cheering when some Jerry plane was hit and the pilot was having his arse burnt off, or parachuting into the Bay of Naples to die of typhoid.

We became friendly with one Franco and his family. He was a shoe salesman in Naples, forty, excused war duties because of ill health, though when I met his giant wife and six kids I couldn't see the reason. She had bosoms like the London Planetarium and was feeding not only her own baby, but wet nursing her neighbours'.

We are invited to partake of the meagre fare. (The last meagre fare I had was a cheap day return to Brockley: Groucho Marx.) Mussels! All bigger than mine. And garlic, phew! Franco's brothers are musicians; they play the mandolin and guitar. I thought they'd like to hear some jazz, so I strummed and sang 'When my sugar walks down the street'. They asked for a translation which was 'Quando mia sucro passegiare fondo la strada, tutti i piccoli ucelli andato tweet tweet tweet' or, 'When my sugar ration walks down the street, it is attended by little birds going tweet tweet tweet.' They liked my Players cigarettes. In exchange they offer me the local Italian brand. I forget the name, I think it was Il Crap.

The village had its resident tart who traded on the outskirts of the town. Her pimp stood outside and shouted: 'Thees way, twenty cigarette you fuck-a my seester.'

'Sister?' said Bronx. 'She looks more like his grand-mother.'

'I think for twenty fags he'd let you fuck 'im,' says Rogers.


## Romance One

It was in the New Army Welfare Rest and Recreation Centre, a large rambling Victorian affair at the top of the village, that I found . . . romance! I had never myself ever had a large rambling Victorian affair, but now, one of the Italian girls serving at the tea bar takes my eye. Arghhh! You've heard of Mars Bars? Forget 'em. She's a ringer for Sophia Loren but six inches shorter and six inches further out. Troubles never come singly, and neither did hers. She likes me, can I have tea with her? There is a smell of burning hairs. I said yes from the waist down. 4 o'clock tomorrow? Si!

I spent all day getting ready. Finally I apply Anzora hair goo and finger-wave my hair. I look lovely. I 'borrow' the jeep and drive to the address. What's this? A magnificent Romano-Greek styled villa; it must be wrong, no, it's right. I drive up the circular drive through embossed iron gates. The great double door: I gently bang the brass hand-shaped knocker. I've only just arrived and there I am with my hand on her knocker.

A suave white-coated grey-haired flunkey opens the door: 'Ah meester Meeligan.' He knows my real title! 'Please come in, the Contessa is waiting.' Contessa? I follow him down a cool marble-floored hall, the walls hung with oil paintings broken by wall consoles. He opens the door into a large gasping-with-light room. The decor is Louis XVI with Baroque gilt furniture. 'She' is sitting against the far wall on a buttoned couch, a fine white cotton dress to the knee (Arghhhhhhh!) brown satin legs (Arghhhh!) fine topless sandals cross laced up her leg (Arghhhhhhhhh!). Her hair is loose on her shoulder (Arrrrghh!), in her hand she holds an Arum lily that she is waving under her nose (Arghhhhhhhhhhhh!) She has been practising this all day. I

40

take off my hat to show her my fine Anzora goo hair-set stuck with flies. 'Hello and arghhhhhhh,' I say.

'Seet here,' she says. (Arghhhhhhhh!) She pats the Louis XIV couch to which I lower my Milligan trousers. It's all too much. She speaks in slow purring tones. (Arghhhhhhhh!)She is very laid back or is it that I'm leaning forward. She asks me what 'Spike' means. I tell her, I mean business. Her family goes back six hundred years, where do mine go back to? I tell her they go back to 50 Riseldine Road, Brockley.

Tea is served on a silver service – how many spoons can I get in my pocket? I ask her where her parents are; they are stopping at Eboli. I tell her I will stop at nothing. Yes, she *is* a Countess. Have I ever been to Eboli? No, I have been to Penge, Sidcup, but not to Eboli. She has heard me tinkering on the piano at the Centre, she likes jazz, will I play her piano? I bluff my way through 'A Foggy Day in London town'. She claps her hands. 'Whatees that?' I tell her: 'It's a piano, don't you remember, you asked me to play it.' The flunkey arrives, it's time for me to depart, la Contessa has another appointment. Blast. 'Can you come see me again?' Yes I can, but can we try a different room next time. I shake hands. It's like a cool perfumed sponge cake. (Argggggggg!)

I'm back at camp lying on my bed smoking, nay steaming, thinking of her. I am besieged with military questions: 'Did I get it?' No I didn't. How far did I get? The piano. What is it about the British soldier? He will knock off a German machine-gun nest single-handed and never say a word about it, but if he knocks off some poor innocent scrubber, he gives you every little nitty gritty detail. I don't get it, as in this case I didn't.

I've caught it. Wait. You don't *catch* bronchitis. I mean you don't chase it up the street with a butterfly net. No. Bronchitis catches you. So, a bronchitis had caught me. It was suffering from me very badly, I had given the poor thing a high temperature, so I had to get my bronchitis to a hospital. No. 104 General at Nocera. Bingo! You've won the

Golden Enema! Another ward, blue jim-jams, female nurses, and mossy nets to stop them dive-bombing. That night I was delirious, but people couldn't tell the difference.

## Diary: April 13

Feeling better. Wrote to mother giving list of my post-war underwear stock.

I go on record that April 16 is my birthday. 'Given extra medicine as a treat.'

Now dear reader, mystery.

## Diary: April 21

'Bert says his leg is getting better.' Now I don't remember Bert or his leg. So, if nothing else, the reader will know that on April 21 1944, Bert's leg is getting better. By now I'd say it was totally better and he's snuffed it.

My bronchitis is better and I can take it back to camp.

## Necrophiles

Outside our camp was the walled cemetery. Alas! the grounds are overgrown with wartime neglect or is it grass? Latins lavish more attention and emotion on their dead than we do. Every headstone has a photograph of the departed. What was ghoulishly interesting were the wall graves, immured with a glass panel to show the departed. One was stunningly macabre: the body of a girl of eighteen buried in 1879 in her bridal gown. The hair was red and had grown after death, as had her fingernails, filling the space like Indian candy floss. The headstones abound with grisly warnings: 'As I am now, so will you be.' Why does the church allow these nasty after-death threats? Why not go the whole hog?

Nasty things are happening – some of the loonies are digging up the graves, or breaking the glass and knocking off the rings. (In the case of bankruptcy break glass?) Jock Rogers is horrified. 'Och, this'll get us a terrible name.' Terrible name? How about Tom Crabs or Doris Herpes? Dick Scratcher?

Private Andrews is more suspicious. 'They're fuckin' the stiffs.' Surely not. 'Aye, they're not after the jewellery, they're after a fuck.' It wasn't so, but we didn't want to spoil Andrews' fun. He was an argumentative bugger, especially on sport. He was a fitba' freak and when he found I liked rugby, gave me hell.

'It's fer bleedin' snobs Jamie, and that ball, like a bloody duck's egg, no wonder you ha' to carry the bloody thing.'

I still wasn't a well person. In May I had three bad depressions. I had heard via the grapevine that some of my mates from 19 Battery were having leave at Amalfi, just an hour up the road. I asked 'Trickcyclist' if I could go and see them, but he said no, we were not to leave the confines of Baiano. It was nonsense. Now I realize I could have gone and taken the quinciquonces. Depressed by the decision, I went straight out, got smashed, came back late, got into the Nissen hut, bolted the door, went on drinking and shouted abuse. Finally I cut my face with a razor blade then fell asleep, all done for effect, a cri de coeur. They broke down the door and took me to the sick bay. When I awoke, Private Shepherd gave me some pills that sent me off again. His exact words were: 'Take these yer daft bugger.' However a letter written at the time showed me to be quite lucid.

MY DEAR DAD,

SORRY TO HAVE DELAYED IN ANSWERING YOUR LAST LETTER,BUT WORK IN THIS OFF
OFFICE IS HINDS HIGH.I NEARLY DROPPED DOWN WITH SHOCK WHEN YOU TOLD ME THAT DES
WAS NOW IN THE ULSTER RIFLES,UP TO THEN I HAD NO IDEA HE WAS EVEN ON THE VERGE
OF JOINING THE ARMY....BUT INFANTRY,THATS NO JOKE,BELIVE ME,IN THIS THEATERE
THE INFANTRY GET ALL THE MUCK,KNOWING DESMONDS PSYCHOLOGICAL CHARACTER AS I DO
IT IS OBVIOUS HE WILL NEVER STICK IT,IF HE COMES OUT HERE I WILL MAKE IT MY
DUTY TO CLAIM HIM,PRETTY SHARP.AS YOU ALREADY KNOW I AM NOW DOWNGRADED TO BI,
FOR THE DURATION,THAT MEANS MY RETURN TO ENGLAND IN ONE PIECE IS ENSURED.
STILL IVE DONE MY BIT ,IVE NEVER SHIRKED MY DUTY,I WOULD STILL BE UP THERE
NOW , BUT THAT SHELL BURST SO CLOSE THAT IT DID MORE DAMAGE TO MY NERVOUS
SYSTEM THAN MY PHYSICAL SELF.STILL IM GETTING BETTER NOW,BUT STILL SUFFER
FROM DEPRESSIONS,WHICH MAKE ME UNBEARBLE AS A COMPANION.TIME IS THE ONLY
DOCTOR,AND OF COURSE MYSELF.WELL DAD HOW IS THE OLD WAR HORSE,I WAS DISSAPOINTED
TO HEAR THAT YOU BOOK COULD NOT BE PRINTED , THE SHORTAGE OF PAPER YOU SAY,IS
IT A BOOK THAT WILL KEEP TILL POST WAR ? OR IS IT A MOOD OF THE MOMENT? GIVE
ME A FEW MORE DETAILS, ABOUT SAME.LILY WRITES REGULAR,AND SO DO ALL MY FRIENDS.
I HAVE LEARNT A LITTLE ITALIAN,AND CAN CARRY ON A REASONABLE CONVERSATION WITH
THE LOCAL NATIVES....ALL ITALIANS CAN SING,KIDS,GRANDMOTHERS,FATHERS,DUSTMEN,
ALL SING..I HAVE BEEN TO SOME FIRST CLASS OPERAS SINCE BEING BASE DEPOTED,
AND THEY WERE TRULY MAGNIFIQUE MON PERE,. THE FOOD IS VERY GOOD IN THIS CAMP
EGGS FOR BREAKFAST EVERY DAY,A CINEMA NEAR BY, A SMALL SWIMMING POOL,AND
A CANTEEN WHICH IS LOCATED IN A LOVLEY VILLA,ADJOINING A GARDEN,IN THIS GARDEN
A RATHER ATTRACTIVE BAND PLAY ITALIAN FOLK MUSIC DURING THE EVENINGS,IT IS VERY
PLEASENT.THERE IS ALSO A QUITE ROOM WHERE ONE CAN WRIT , STUDY ECT.A TRAIN
SERVICE IS AVAILABLE TO BIG TOWNS,AND TRAVELLING ON ONE OF THESE IS A REAL
EXPERIENCE,EVERY ONE TALKS ALOUD SINGS FIGHTS AND IF THE ROOM IS FULL,THEY
JUST HANG ON THE OUTSIDE,ALL VERY UNSTAID AS COMPARED WITH ENGLISH TRAVEL.
TAKEN ON THE WHOLE ITALY IS VERY VERY ATTRACTIVE,THE DIVINE COAST FOR INSTANCE

A STRETCH OF COAST FROM SALERNO TO SORRENTO,THER IS SCENERY THAT HAS INSPIRED
POETS PAINTERS MUSICIANS FOR CENTURIES,IT IS STEEPED IN HISTORY,I HAVE RECORDED
MANY INTERESTING FACT ABOUT THESE QUAINT PLACES I HAVE VISITED,DURING MY LEAVE
PERIODS IN THIS COUNTRY.MY POST CARD COLLECTION IS NOW ENOURMOUS,I'M SURE YOU
WILL BE DELIGHTED TO SEE MY COLLECTION.I HAVE ALSO MANAGED TO OBTAIN A PIECE
OF MOSAIC FROM ONE OF THE VILLAS IN RUINED POMPEII.

(AT THIS STAGE YOU MUST EXCUSE THE ERRATIC SPACING BUT THIS MISSIVE HAS BEEN
REMOVED FROM THE TYPEWRITE  TO ALLOW THE DISPATCHES OF WAR TO TAKE PRECEDENCE),
ANY HOW POMPEII....I SPENT THREE DAYS OF MY FOUR DAY LEAVE IN THIS ENCHANTING TOWN
OF YESTERYEAR,I TOOK PARTICULAR NOTE OF THE architecure ARCHITICTURE OF THAT IDOM,AND STRANGE
TO SAY THE COUNTRY BUILDINGS OF TO DAY( IN ITALY ) ARE DEFINATELY A PROTOTYPE,OF
POMPEII'S VILLAS.THE FARMERS OUT HERE ARE MASTERS OF THEIR CRAFT,STILL EMPLOYING
METHODS CONSIDERED ANCIENT BY OUR STANDARDS,BUT NEVER THE LESS PRODUCING THE SAME
FULL HARVEST.THE LATIN'S ARE NOT LIVING A LIFE BASED ON THE GLORIFICATION IN MY PAST
FEW LINES ..ON THE CONTRARY,I SHOULD SAY BY MERE OPTICAL DEDUCTION,THAT 30 % OF
ITALIAN FAMILIES ARE BARELY EXISTING.THE REST LIVE ON EITHER BLACK MARKET,THEIR
WITS OR WORKING FOR THE ANGLO-AMERICAN FORCE.I HAVE A REALLY GOOD FRIEND IN THE LOCAL
TOWN..HE IS A FAMILY MAN,A CHARMING AND FAITHFUL WIFE(A RARITY IN ENGLAND) AND
5 BEAUTIFUL CHILDREN,ONE OF WHICH(ANNA BY NAME)I AM VERY MUCH ATTACHED TOO,SHE
IA 5 YEARS OF AGE,A TYPICAL LATIN,BROWN EYES THAT HAVE PATHOS,SINCERETY,WARMTH
AND ALL THAT GO TO MAKE THE FEATURES WORTHY OF THEIR ROMAN ANCESTORS,FRANCO HAS
  3 BROTHERS,ALL THINK THE WORLD OF ME,THEY ARE MUSICAL,EACH BEING A COMPETENT SOLOIST
ON THE GUITAR,MANDOLIN AND VIOLIN..THEY WERE VERY THRILLED TO KNOW AND HEAR ME PLAY
THE GUITAR,I SPEND EVERY EVENING AT THEIR HOME,WITH THE ERROR TRADITONAL VINO BLANCA
(WHITE WINE) AND FRUIT THAT WOULD DRIVE AN ENGLISH HOUSE WIFE OFF HER HEAD WITH JOY.
WELL DAD YOU HAVE HEARD ENOUGH FOR TO NIGHT(THE CANDLE IS RUNNING LOW) I MUST
FINI POURA SA SARA. AREA FER TEACHI(SEEIN YA)

                    YOUR AFFECTIONATE SON

                         TERRY.




P.S. PLEASE PASS THIS LETTER ON TO MUM.

                    T.M.

A stream that runs through the camp has been dammed and a swimming hole is the result. I will recount an incident with one of the more advanced loonies. 'Tis evening, and Milligan takes to the waters; there approaches a loony. The conversation I remember almost to the word.

LOONY: Hey you.
ME: Yes.
LOONY: Hey you. Come here. Come here.

> (*I could hear him perfectly from where I was, but I thought perhaps he had something to give me. I drew to the side.*)

ME: Yes?
LOONY: What's it like in there?
ME: (*puzzled*) What's it like?
LOONY: Aye.
ME: Well, it's wet.
LOONY: Oh, it's wet, is it?
ME: Has that put you off?
LOONY: Is it warm?
MY: Yes.
LOONY: It's wet and warm, eh?
ME: Yes.
LOONY: Is it comfortable?
ME: Yes.

(It would appear he wants personal references for the swimming hole.)

ME: Yes, it's very comfortable, it fits well under the arms, it's not too tight in the crutch, and the water reaches down to below the feet. It's a light brown colour, you don't need buttons and it doesn't crease.

He stood still for a moment, then without a word of thanks, went his way whistling all the while.

## Sport

Captain Peters is of a mind that we are in need of exercise. 'Football! Phnut!' The camp is divided into four teams – Red, Blue, White, Yellow. The teams were up to twenty a side. I played for the Reds. I never saw the ball, but I heard it several times. Getting past two goalies presented difficulties, especially as they threatened you if you tried to score a goal. 'You score and I'll kill you, you bastard!' Still, it was fun. Athletics presented a problem as there was no track. Owing to the terrain, all races had to be run in a straight line. This was OK for the Dash but the mile was a disaster. Records? Forget it; over the stony pot-holed track it took the winner of the 100 yards 20 seconds! The mile took a quarter of an hour and we had to send a truck out to bring them back. The Marathon was cancelled. As Peters said, 'We'd never see them again.' The prizes were ideal for those trying to get fit. Fags.

## June. A Posting

Ah! That Italian summer in the Campania. The mornings, the cool air touching the face like an eider feather, the dawn light under the tent flap vivifying the moment, the aroma of dew on earth, the distant cockerel, the sound of the old guard standing down, the clank of the early morning tea bucket. Long before we rose the trundling of ox carts to the fields and the 'Aie!' of the calling herdsmen, all this and the lung-bursting coughing of Private Andrews.

'Who's a lucky lad then?' says Sergeant Arnolds.

I pause at my desk and answer: 'A lucky lad is the Duke of Windsor now soaking up sea and sun as the Governor of Bermuda.' No, no, the lucky boy is me. He throws me a document. From this camp of a thousand loonies I am being posted to the Officers' Club, Portici, as a wine steward. The word gets round. Milligan is leaving!!

The night before I left, Reg Bennett, Jock Rogers, Bronx Weddon, Private Andrews and I had a farewell party at the

Welfare Centre. It was eggs and chips and red wine. Reg played the piano, I played the trumpet, then into the back garden to hear the Italian orchestra playing old Neapolitan Airs – 'Lae ther piss tub down bab' ('Lay that Pistol down, Babe').

'The place won't be the same without you,' says a tearful Reg Bennett. I tell him it wasn't the same *with* me. We stagger home by a hunter's moon, our shadows going before us on the silver ribbon of a road. Me, at an Officers' Club!

'I wonder what they'll make me,' I said.

'They'll make you an offer,' says Bronx

## The Officers' Club, Portici

It was a large splendid classical-style villa on the main road. I walked up a tessellated path, then right up marble steps with Venetian balustrades into a large white foyer, which had pedestalled busts of Apollo, Hermes, Aristotle and several etcs. In a large dining-room I am intercepted by a short squat thick-set Corporal of the Black Watch, complete in clan kilt. He is the image of Jerry Collona.

'I'm Gunner Milligan I –'

He pounces in. 'Ahhyes, you've come at an awkward time.'

'I could come back . . . after the war.'

No, follow him. Through an arched annexe into a sumptuous room, the beds are on a three-foot raised platform in the middle, surrounded by a Roman-style wooden railing in the St Andrew's Cross design. 'It's how the Romans used to sleep, raised up,' he explains. 'That's my bed, use the mossy-net at night and take Mepacrin.' He is Corporal Tom Ross. 'You can call me Tom, except near officers.' Right, he can call me Spike, except near railings. He is from the 51st Highland Division. Had I heard of them? Yes, we called them the 'Hydraulics' because they would lift anything. He too was bomb-happy. 'Alamein, it were tue much fer me.' I told him not to worry, it was too much for Rommel as well.

I met the staff. The cook, Franco (all Italian cooks not

48

called Maria are Francos in Italy), two serving girls, Rosa and Maria (all Marias not called Rosa are called Marias in Italy), girl secretary Bianca, Italian barman Carlo (all Italians not called Franco are Carlos except the Pope). The officer in charge is Lieutenant Oliver Smutts, bomb-happy, balding, with an Adam's apple which looks like a nose further down; slim, as are his chances of promotion. He interviewed me. I was to be receptionist and wine waiter.

SMUTTS: Do you know much about wine, Milligan?
MILLIGAN: Yes sir, I get pissed every night.

The club is open from midday till the wee hours. It closes when either the guests or the staff collapse. A 'Gypsy' band plays for dancing; the leader is Enrico Spoleto, who turns out to be the Town Major's batman, Eric Collins. In his black trousers, white shirt and red bandanna, he looked as much like a gypsy as Mel Brooks looked like Tarzan.

## DRAMATIS PERSONAE

| | |
|---|---|
| Lieutenant Oliver Smutts . . | Ruler of a marbled drinking palace |
| Corporal Tom Ross . . . . . . . | An untreated Scots Eunuch |
| Gunner Milligan . . . . . . . . . | Buttons |
| Maria . . . . . . . . . . . . . . . . | Virgin in Waiting |
| Rosa . . . . . . . . . . . . . . . . | Virgin not waiting too long |
| Carlo. . . . . . . . . . . . . . . . | Barman/Mafia |
| Bianca. . . . . . . . . . . . . . . | Hand maiden to Pasha Smutts |
| Franco . . . . . . . . . . . . . . | Cook and resident Sex Maniac |

Various gardeners, scrubbers, dustmen.

The job is bliss, except! Pasha Smutts is jealous. Bianca, his fancy, fancies Buttons. Was it my fault that I was lovely? Lots of fun and games with Maria and Rosa. Breakfast is in bed! Brought by Rosa or Maria. Maria made a point of whipping the bedclothes off to examine my condition. I never failed her. It was a good Rabelaisian start to the day.

My duties are to make out the menus, check the wine stocks, and release anyone imprisoned in them. Apart from the gypsy orchestra, there's still a lot of fiddling. Tom balances the books so well we all pocket five hundred lire a week. The evil cook will do anything for fags except his wife. Rosa lays the tables and Tom lays Rosa. I sit at the door and book the officers in. It was a paid membership club, with a tendency to not remembership to pay. Like Groucho Marx said: 'Never lend people money, it gives 'em amnesia . . .'

## The Dancing Officers

The terrace is cleared for these gyrations. Most of the partners are WREN or ATS Officers and the occasional upper class Iti scrubber. Spoleto and his 'Gypsies' make woeful attempts to play 'Moonlight Serenade', 'One o'clock Jump', and 'Chattanooga Choo Choo'. The trouble is the partially deaf Italian drummer of seventy who has no damper on his bass drum so that it booms round the room like a cannon; but we are grateful for it when Spoleto takes a vocal in an appalling nanny-goat voice: 'There'll be BOOM BOOM over the BOOM BOOM of Dover To BOOM BOOM just you wait and BOOM BOOM.' Thank God they never played the Warsaw Concerto.

Dancing. There are none worse than those swaying pump-handled Hooray Henrys. I watched the agonized gyrations of the two dancers' feet, neither pair knowing what instructions it was supposed to be receiving. The male feet getting vague messages, the female feet immediately having to adjust to their bidding. The female is being backed up like a coal lorry. To vary this the male suddenly tries to revolve her round him, ending up with Barley Twist legs and shattered knees. The female legs are now at the rear of the male legs, the male unwinds his Barley Twist legs bringing the poor female's legs back again, and the coal lorry style continues.

There can be no enjoyment in it at all, but it has to be done.

Through the warm night Spoleto and his 'Gypsies' batter through 'Little Brown Jug'. I tell Tom, 'He thinks he's Glenn Miller.' Tom says he's more like 'Max Fuckin' Miller'. It had to be done.

Wow! Gentry! General Alexander and his retinue breeze in for an after-dinner drink. Immaculate in starched KDs, he was in a, shall-we-say, 'flushed' mood; he had just seen the Anzio breakout, the fall of Rome and the news of D-Day. This was a celebration. I admired him until he too started barley twisting his legs on the floor. His laughing retinue was last to leave. As I handed him his hat, he said 'What do you do?'

'I hand hats to departing officers,' I replied.

He smiled and barley twisted his way out. A great soldier, a terrible dancer.

## Music Maestro Please

Spoleto had given me the address of a Professor Fabrizzi. He lived in a seedy villa in Resina, a town built over the city of Herculaneum. He was about seventy and used to play the harp in the San Carlo Orchestra and I could see that it wouldn't be long before he would be playing it again. He had long white snowy hair, a gaunt shrunken smiling face and two deep-set brown eyes. Harmony and counterpoint? Of course, 500 lire an hour. 'Harmony is not easy,' he said. At 500 lire a go I agreed. His 'study' was lined with books on music and gardening. Perhaps I could learn harmony and tree growing. 'Professor Milligan will now play his tree! The compostion is in A Minor, the tree is in A garden.'

The lessons start. 'You see dis black a notes.' Can I see it? I ask him is he an optician or a music teacher? That is the note of C. I knew that. 'The notes on the line-a above is E.' I knew that. He told me how the scales went. I knew that as well. Something else I knew, I was being conned. I went away richer in life's experience and he richer by two thousand lire. I watched as he counted every single lire. It's the little things that count and he was one of them.

One night after closing I hie me to the city of Herculaneum. The dead city lies sightless in the bay light of a Neapolitan moon. I walk through the unattended entrance: 'Vietato ingresso'. The city is like Catford, after dark. Dead. I walk along the sea front from which the seas have departed that day in AD 79. This was Bournemouth to Pompeii's Blackpool. Here people sat on summer's nights drinking wine and eating figs from water-filled bowls. Now all gone. Ghosts, ghosts, ghosts.

> Ohhh, Herculaneum City
> Ohhh what a terrible pity
> All of you had gone
> Except a little tiny bitty.

Back at the billet I awake Tom.
'Who's that?' he snuffled.
'Errol Flynn.'
'You silly bugger.'
'A man can dream, can't he?'
Where had I been, and did I get it?
'Nay, I'm as pure as the driven snow. I've been to Herculaneum.'

---

COURT FOR THE IGNORANT

JUDGE: What is a Herculaneum?

QC TARLO: Herculaneum my lord is a place where any free-born slave can go and Hercu-his-laneum.

JUDGE: Oh, and in Hercuing-his-laneum, what benefits are derived?

QC TARLO: The swelling on the Blurzon is much reduced.

JUDGE: What is a Blurzon.

QC TARLO: It is a small hairy area at the back of the knee where Armenian shepherds crack their nuts.

---

Oh, what's Herculaneum?

By day I have quite a lot of time on my hands; I also have it on my legs, elbows and shins. There was a lot of it about.

## A Colonel Intervenes

Yes! One evening as I sat at the reception desk varnishing walnuts and cracking them behind my knee, a man in a jeep approached. He was to be instrumental in changing my life. By instrumental I don't mean he was playing the trombone, no. The man is Colonel Startling Grope, a reddish middle-aged man, portly, used to good living, hair cuts, Horlicks, thin legs and suede desert boots. He had a body that appeared to have been inflated, and the air was escaping. When he signed in he shot me a glance full of meaning that I knew not the meaning of.

Later that night, as he and his cronies are departing, all so pissed you could hear the cistern flushing, he enquires: 'What do you do here?' I tell him on a good day I give General Alexander his hat. Otherwise I try not to whistle the Warsaw Concerto. He is intrigued; as he should be. I am quite lovely. Seriously, I'm a wine steward and resident manic depressive. 'How would you like to come and work for me as a wine steward and resident manic depressive?' I say yes. Why? Because I have been brought up to feel inferior to everybody: priests, doctors, bank managers and officers were all Gods. To say no to them was a mortal sin punishable by 500 Hail Marys and an overdraft.

Within a week a jeep arrives and takes me away. The girls all cried and the men cheered. Looking through my diary I found the note I made at the time.

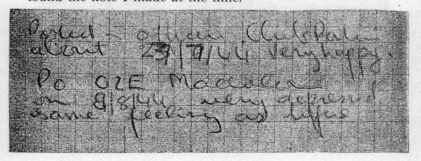

Translation. 'Posted 02E Maddaloni on 8/8/44. Very depressed, same feeling as before.'

So! I was feeling myself like I had before, a duty that until recently had been performed by Maria.

What was happening to me? I didn't want to be a Manic Depressive Wine Waiter in Italy! I wanted to be a Manic Depressive Harry James in Catford. Why did a poofy Colonel need a wine waiter???

The jeep driver is an ex-paratrooper. Ted Noffs gives me the first warning: 'Yew wanna watch yer arsole wiv 'im.' My God, a Brown Hatter! We drive in silence. Speedo says 33 mph, petrol half full, all exciting stuff. Right now my last exciting stuff, Rosa, was back at Portici. An hour's dusty drive with night approaching. A sign: MADDALONI.

*Maddaloni on a Good Day*

'Not far now,' said Noffs. 'We korls it Mad'n'lonely, ha ha.' He was such a merry fellow, a fellow of infinte jest and a cunt. We enter a town and slow down outside a faceless three-storeyed municipal school. Turning left by its side we come to a rear back lot with a line of tents and parked vehicles. Noffs stops outside a ten-man tent. 'This is yourn.' I thank him and lug my kit into the tent which has an electric light, brighter than the three slobs lying on their beds, smoking and staring. These are khaki skivvies, the play-things of the commissioned classes. One is Corporal Rossi, London Italian Cockney. 'You the new wine steward?' Yes. He's the head barman. I'll be working under him. That's my bed. I ask all the leading questions:

> a Where's the cook house?
> b The NAAFI?
> c The Karzi?
> d What day was free issue?
> e Any ATS?

e) No, there's no ATS but there's scrubbers in town who do it for ten fags. There's 'one that does it for two but she gives you a dose'. This is the stuff that never reaches Official War Histories, folks!

I find the canteen in the main barrack block (more of it later), have a glass of red wine and a cheese sandwich. The place is full, and soon so am I. I don't know anybody and nobody wants to know me, but then I haven't been on tele-vision yet! The red wine sets me up for bed. Back under bloody canvas yet again. Like Robert Graves I thought I'd said Goodbye to All That; instead it was Hello to all This! I slept fitfully, sometimes I slept unfitfully. Variety is the spice of life, or if you live in a after-shave factory, the Life of Spice.

Raffia Party Hats. I was given orders like 'Tins to be smoothed' and 'Bar top to be desplintered'. There I was at dawn with a dopey driver driving around the streets of Caserta buying cabbages, potatoes, figs and oranges, lentils and the whole range of fresh foods for O2E Officers' Mess. Another Fine Mess I'd gotten into. Shagged out by mid-afternoon, I was then put on bar duties for the evening, serving a crowd of pissy Hooray Henrys. By the amount of drink and smoke around they must long since have died of lung cancer or cirrhosis. Disaster. The bar phone rings; they want a Major Bastard. That's how they pronounced it.

'Phone call for Major Bastard,' I yell above the din.

A man purple with rage and halitosis snatches the phone: 'Bass-*tard*, you Bastard,' he hissed. He was a real Bass-tard!

I was making a cock-up of the job. Not that I couldn't do it, I didn't want to.

'The Colonel wants to see you,' says Rossi. OK, if he looks through that window, he'll get a glimpse of me desplintering the bar.

'Look Milligan,' says Major Startling Grope. We are in his office. 'The Sergeant says you aren't very good at your job.'

'He's a liar, sir. I'm bloody useless at my job. I could lose us the war.'

He laughed. How am I at clerking? I don't know.

'How are you at figures?'

'Terrible, you should see the women I go out with.'

'Look, Milligan, give it a try. If you don't like it, we can try something else.' Like Suicide. OK.

I work for him in 'O' Branch in the school building. A large airy office with a Sergeant Hallam, a mild-mannered poof. Then a clerk, Private Len Arrowsmith, a small lively amusing lad; then me at the bottom of the heap as filing clerk. We each have a separate desk. It's cushy. I just get files, give files and take the files back; the job has all the magic of an out-of-order phone box. It's OK to sleep in the office provided bedding is hidden during the day! So I move in and join Arrowsmith.

'You'll like it here,' says Len. 'At night you have a lovely view of the typewriter.'

**Romance**

So far Sergeant Hallam has always carried the files to the Colonel. But I'm lovelier. So now it's me.

56

Announcement over the interphone. 'Send Milligan in with File X.' The Colonel is 'getting to know me'. I was going through what girls go through with in the initial chatting-up process.

'What is your – er – do sit down, Milligan, you can dispense with rank.'

'I haven't any rank to dispense with, sir.'

'You can call me Stanley.'

'Yes sir, Stanley.'

'What's your first name?'

'Spike, Stanley, sir.'

'Spike? That's not your real name.'

'No, my real name is Terence.'

At the mention of the name his eyes lit up with love.

'Terence,' he lisped. 'Yes, that's better, Terence, that's what I'll call you.' Like Private Noffs said: 'Watch yer arsole.'

I had not forgotten my trumpet. In the evening I'd

02E *Dance Band, August–September 1944, each man a master of posing.* Piano: *Sgt. S. Britton;* Bass: *L/Bdr. L. Prosser;* Drums: *Pte. 'Chick' Chitty;* Guitar: *Phil Phillips;* 1st Trumpet: *Gnr. S. Milligan;* 2nd Trumpet: *Pte. G. Wilson;* 1st Alto: *Sgt. H. Carr;* 2nd Alto: *Pte. J. Manning;* Tenor: *Pte. J. Buchanan*

practise in the office. Those notes that echoed round
Maddaloni's fair streets were to lead me to fame, fortune,
overdraft, VAT, Income Tax, mortgages, accountants,
solicitors, house agents, nervous breakdown and divorce. It
starts with a tall thin, bald, moustachioed Sergeant Phil
Phillips. He leads the 02E band. Will I play for them? Yes,
yes, yes, yes. Here is a recollection of those days by the bass
player L/Bdr Len Prosser, who is now, according to his psychiatrist, the President of the United States.

LEN PROSSOR'S RANDOM REMINISCENCES OF ITALY - 1944 - 1946

The 02E Dance Orchestra started out playing for dancing in the hall at Maddaloni
Barracks, later playing "in the pit" for variety shows each Saturday night and
on occasion during the week. For some shows the band would be on stage in the
tradition of "show bands," set up in tiers. Recalled is one particular Saturday
evening when several of the band members had been celebrating some promotions
in the cellar bistro known as "Aldo's" in the village of Maddaloni Inferiore
(very), partaking of the local, very sickly and thick version of Vermouth,
imbibed from cut-down beer and wine bottles. I was one of them; I am not certain
that you, Spike, were there, but it was possible, since I recall that at some
time in your career you were awarded the stripes of a sergeant, and that was most
likely the time.    When it came to near curtain time for the show, which the
band was to open from behind the tabs with Dorsey's Song of India, we left Aldo's
and wended our way up to the hall feeling rather the worse for the wine.
    Drummer Chick Chitty and I were on the top tier, setting up our gear, when
I staggered and fell, bass and all, down the tiers. Chick tried to grab me but
managed to tumble down also. We ended up among the saxophones; were not hurt,
but my bass was punctured in the side by Harry Carr's sax-stand.
    The uniforms the band wore, I recall were the result of your initiative.
The trousers were khaki drill dyed black; the jackets were of white duck and
made by a Neapolitan tailor, I believe, although somewhere in my memory I remember visiting a laundry in Naples for a "fitting." Anyway, we all felt and
looked better for being able to wear this approximation of a civilian band
uniform, and soon after we started wearing it our bookings began to come in thick
and fast. We played for the American Red Cross in Caserta and elsewhere (enjoy-
ing some great food such as meat balls and rice; a welcome change from our diet
in the barracks). We also played at the Palace in Caserta for dances, and for
the same purpose at the Palace in Naples, which you will recall was a huge
NAAFI when we were there. Gracie Fields was then living on Capri, and she would
be a regular visitor to the Naples NAAFI, performing on every visit and eventually
becoming something of a bore to the fellows regularly visiting the place. The
band played each Thursday evening for an open-air dance in the orange grove in
the centre of Maddaloni; many American officers would be there, some of them were
musicians who liked to sit in with the band. We also travelled to other places
and performed for American and British units in concert. These included a two-
week trip to Rome to play in the NAAFI there, which in normal times was a most
modern department store. I remember your being in this place, Spike, up in one
of the rooms trying out material on a piano.  The band played in the evenings
for dancing at that place, and in the daytime we roamed about the city. You and I
billeted together on that occasion and both of us were very upset at finding
some small children rummaging for food in a garbage can (not that this was at all
unusual). We managed to "steal" some sandwiches for them and you gave them some
cigarettes, also, that they presumably could trade for something edible.
    One big fillip to our enthusiasm at that that time was a gesture on the part
of the Americans for whom we played; they gave us a chance to visit their Post
Exchange and choose some new instruments and a number of orchestrations. That
was in Caserta.  This brought some great band numbers such as Woody Herman's

<u>Apple Honey</u> and several Glenn Miller orchestrations. Our first run-though of
<u>String of Pearls</u> provided a memory of Jim Manning (2nd alto and a regular Army
band musician) coming to a solo part inscribed "as played by Ernie Caceres."
It comprised a series of minin-value chords written in notation. Jim played the
top minin in each case and the rest of us dissolved in laughter. Jim took um-
brage, saying, "If you don't like it, get fuckin' Ernie Casseries to play it."
And then he walked out of the hall where we were practising.

Do you remember ~~our~~ band room in the barracks? It was furnished with ~~rugs~~
and armchairs and suchlike stolen from places where we had been playing, such as
officers' clubs in the locality. It was a simple matter to load such items into
the truck, with our gear, at the end of the evening. It was in this band room
that I first realised how great you were with the guitar, finger-style. I can
remember your lying on the rug with the guitar on your chest, playing ~~some~~
extempore thing that had all of us quiet and listening. Even a young ATS girl
named Gay Endars, who was a singer with the band and a girl-friend of Stan
Britton's, was completely enraptured by that moment. And I don't suppose you
will even remember the incident.

Another Glenn Miller memory: The Welsh lad, Harry Carr, lead alto (he looked
like a cadaverous version of Engelbert Humperdinck) playing the chart of <u>Moon-
light Serenade</u> for the first time with tears streaming down his face from the
sheer emotion of playing the orchestration and its soaring lead alto part. Harry,
a carpenter in civilian times was, as I recall, a pretty good musician who also
played piano quite brilliantly, but had only one piano piece in his repertoire:
the verse of <u>Stardust</u>.

Also remembered are other fellows in the band such as guitarist Bert Munday.
Nicest fellow you could meet, and pretty well known prewar as a semipro in South
London (his home was at the Oval). I saw him a few times after the war; he died
of leukemia in 1949.

Stan Britton, phlegmatic person and rather heavy-handed pianist from North
London. Easy to get along with and quite knowledgeable musically. I recall that
he put together some 12-bar blues things for the band, calling the chart <u>Madda-
loni Madness</u> when we played "at home," <u>Caserta Capers</u> when played thereat, and
so on et seq.

Another easy-going chap was tenor saxist Charlie Ward; something of a dry
comedian and older than the rest of us. Used to do one vocal, <u>I'm Gonna Get Lit
Up When the Lights Go On in London</u>. Then there was George Wilson, trumpet man
from Huddersfield in Yorkshire, who had but one lung left after being wounded
in North Africa. I saw him several times after the war. He was not in the best
of health and had not played a note since getting out of the army. When he was
with us he had a wonderful look of resignation when you, Spike, would be unable
to play lead (he greatly enjoyed playing second to you). There were a few times
in the Naples area when we would be playing for dancing, when into the hall would
glide a rather attractive ATS girl, who, I remember, would not give you any en-
couragement at all, and yet you were very keen on her. Maybe she was playing
games, but she wouldn't give you a tumble and seemed to take delight in being
there, with you sequestered on the bandstand. Anyway, it got to the point where
you had "lip trouble" each time she appeared; George would see her enter the
hall and begin to take bets on just how many minutes it would be before he had
to take over lead owing to your emotional "lip."

At one time we had a trumpet player named "Judy" Garland, from Nottingham.
When there were three trumpets he'd play the trombone part on his horn. He was
a slight, bespectacled and cheerful lad.

We had other fellows in the band from time to time, but the ones mentioned
above are the musicians best remembered by me.

Of course, at Maddaloni, as things got more organised after the fighting
stopped in Italy, there were other activities. One of these was the drama group
run by a fellow named Lionel Hamilton. This group did Mary Hayley Bell's play,
<u>Men in Shadow</u> as an early effort, and you wrote a satire on this play, calling
it <u>Men-in-Gitis</u>, that was staged a week later for a week's run. It was billed as
"The Goons in Men-in-Gitis". I helped you to prepare the script for this show
(but didn't provide any creative input, I'm sure) in your little cubby-hole room
near the gate of the Maddaloni barracks building. I remember the room well; it
had on the walls pictures of all the "birds" you had known during your Army days,
stretching back to Bexhill-on-Sea. That was my first contact with your "Goons"
concept, and I recall the opening scene and offstage spoken line: "As our play

opens we find Old Pierre, slowly chopping wood by the mill." This line was in the straight version, and was repeated in yours; but in yours, as the curtain was raised, Old Pierre was chopping wood so frantically that the pieces were flying out into the audience, hitting the backdrop and whizzing into the wings. Great stuff. I'll always remember it.

Also recalled is a gag that was pulled, at your behest, in a concert for a British outfit near Naples. You had the compere announce that as a special treat we had secured the "San Carlo Trio" from the Opera House - and the tabs went up to reveal three of us in fright wigs, with backs to audience, ready to play some feeble jazz. The audience, that included some straight aficionados of the opera, registered delight at the announcement and absolute dismay when they saw what we really had for them.

I remember some really joyous times with the band, and with you. Ever since those days I have remained convinced that being in the band saved my sanity in the war years, and I guess that you feel similarly. Also, I have always been certain that dance musicians, and jazz musicians more especially, are really the salt of the earth. As a class they are blessed with a sense of humour (see how many prominent comedians, British and American, were originally in the music business), and are warm and friendly human beings.

The comradeship experienced by men during those years was something most difficult to explain or define in ordinary terms, at least for me. It is a feeling, a connection, hardly understood by women, and I am grateful that I experienced it. But philosophy is not really my line, and so I will not dwell on this aspect of our army days.

I daresay that after this is in the mail to you I will think of other incidents and occasions. However, let this suffice. After all, the things mentioned in this remembrance may be of little use for your biographical purposes. But it is hoped that at least they will provoke your own memories and thus prove of some value.

March 21, 1975

*Len Prosser*

6907 Strathmore Street
Chevy Chase, Maryland
USA

Thank you Len Prosser, a year's subscription to EXIT is on its way.

Now life took on a new meaning. Playing with the band was a bonus. We played from smoky dives to the great Palace of Caserta which housed the Allied Forces Headquarters, though it was so far behind the lines it was referred to as the Hind Quarters. We were given a rehearsal room where we tried to keep up with the very advanced band arrangements we bought from the American PX. Playing Woody Herman's arrangement of 'Apple Honey' nearly did for us – the top F's gave rise to cries of 'The truss, bring the truss.' After one appalling run-through, Stan Britton turned to us and said, 'Gentlemen, I suggest we take an early retirement.'

Another disaster was our first attempt at the new-fangled

samba, called 'Brazil'. After three tries, Charlie Ward put his sax down and said, 'The defence rests.' A letter written at the time tells of the good life I was leading.

However, years later I saw a shopping list on the back, showing the penny-pinching life my mother was leading under wartime rationing. 'They also serve . . .' Serves her bloody well right. If she had joined the Army, she wouldn't have suffered so!

My Address:— Gnr. T. A Milligan
954024
G.H.Q. 2 Echelon.
'O' Clerks.
CMF          30 Aug 1944


My Dearest Mum,
                                   just a few lines to accompany
this photograph of my noble self. It was
taken during The fighting S of the Gangliano
River — happy days !!! I am working in a really
comfortable job — and the Col. of the Unit likes
me very much — he said "Milligan — write and
tell your mum that I'm looking after you"
and he certainly does — he is taking me
swimming next sunday — he is a real good
stick — I am clerking — and also a member
of the Orchestra — a very big one 15 players we
play at some real classey dances, with cash —
food & drinks. Tell desmond I will
write soon. Tell dad I've had 3 Parcels
of Books from him — could you send me
(Blades Gillett if possible
(Aspros (headaches eat colds)
(A few Packets of Churchmans No 1 Cigs.
(5 Handkerchiefs.
(Some Talcum Powder if possible
(and cough Lozengers
(and Capsules

That all for now mum
                    tons of Love
          your son Dr.
                    Terry
                    xxxxx

## Dances! Dances!

Dances meant pretty girls and a burning sensation. At a dance in the Caserta ballroom, I fell for – a ridiculous phrase, 'fell for' – no, I didn't pitch forward on my face, but when I saw her I just screamed. She was gliding past the bandstand in another man's arms. I'd only just seen her and she was already being unfaithful to me!! Her name was Sheila Frances, mine was Spike Milligan. Did she come here often, yes, and this was one of them. I try to date her and come up with 1944. I fall for her hook, line and sinker, and several other parts all hanging under the shirt. Blast, she is affianced to a Sergeant. I will try again. Meantime I'll go blind. I climb back on to the bandstand; lots of nudge nudges wink winks.

'There's plenty more fish in the sea, Spike,' says Len Prosser. But I don't want to go out with fish.

## Filing for King and Country!

Files, bloody files, I'm bored with files, so bored I open a new one and slip it into the system. Marked incident at Alexander Barracks. Inside I had typed a memo:

*Statement by Guard Commander
of Incident outside Barracks.*

Sir, on the night of the Twolth of Higust at oooo Dearie me hours, when I heard a sound, 'Pisssssshhhh' it went, I challenged the sound. 'Halt who goes there?' No reply, so I challenged in Italian. 'Halto who goes thereo!' No reply, so I challenged in Aramaic, finally in Chinese, 'Dim Sim, Plancake Loll, Plawn Clackers,' whereupon a shadowy figure drew nigh. It was a Tuna Fish wearing a kilt and clutching a Mandolin. I had not been drinking but I think the Tuna Fish had. I fired a round into its sporran, whereupon it departed in the crouched position. Signed Private Knotts.

The file arrived on Colonel Startling Gropes' table. He added a memo:

'This is one of the most serious cases of seriousness I have read. There must be a full investigation.'

He forwarded the file to Colonel Thompson in 'A' Branch who had a sense of humour and boils. He added to the fun: 'I am forwarding this to Major Bastard for a full medical report.' The file grew to nearly six inches thick and was still circulating when I left.

## A Day Out in a Certain Direction

Colonel Startling Grope to Milligan: 'Would you and Len like to come to Ischia?'

'Yes sir, I'd love an Ischia.'

'Right, Sunday morning 0800. Bathing costume and towel.'

The day. Colonel Startling Grope, Captain Clarke, Len and myself pile on the jeep. 9.10 we arrive at the specially bombed car park on the water front at Naughty Naples. We go on board an awaiting RAF Rescue launch. 'Welcome aboard,' says a silly sea captain, all beard and binoculars. 'Cast off forrard, cast off aft,' whoosh, turbines throb and we head out into the mist-haunted sea. Our two officers are taken below for drinkypoos; we stay on deck and talk to the crew. 'Hello sailor,' I say.

The bay is calm, looking like skimmed oil. We bounce on the surface and the morning mist starts to lift. In twenty minutes looms the soaring purple head of Mount Epomeo. We draw near to the south shore, skilfully entering a little fishing mole amid red and blue fishing boats with the warding-off evil eye on the prows. We heave to as our two officers surface flushed and smiling. We jump ashore. The Colonel misses and plunges his leg up to the groin in the waters. 'Oh bother,' he says, meaning 'Oh fuck.'

With seven dry legs and one wet one, we follow the Colonel up a small path inland that leads us to a bleached white Italo-Moorish villa on the sea. A brief pull on the doorbell; the red mahogany door opens to a small smiling, white-coated, thirty-year-old, blood group Rhesus negative inside leg forty-two, valet. He ushers us in, all the while looking suspiciously at the Colonel's one damp leg. This is the Villa

San Angelo, owned by an Italian Colonello with two dry legs. He is at the moment 'away on business in Naples'. Possibly at this moment, he and two pimps are changing lire into sawdust on the Via Roma.

The Moors have left their mark here: many arches, turquoise tiled floors, latticed screens, Fazan carpets. It is a treasure house of antiques – Majolica Ceramics, Venetian Glass, Inlaid Moorish Muskets, Tapestried Walls. 'Homely isn't it, Terence,' says the Colonel. After a cold buffet of avocado and prawns and wine of the island, our officers retire to sleep. Len and I are directed to the private beach down a few rocky steps. The day is sunny, the sea is like champagne. We plunge into crystal clear waters that in forty years time will be floating with tourist crap and over-population. Lording over the island is Mount Epomeo, hung with a mantle of vineyards and bougainvillaea. Legend has it that the giant Typhoeus lies transfixed beneath it. A punishment for screwing one of the Naiads. I suppose one way of keeping it down is to put a mountain on it.

On this very island Michelangelo used to visit the lady Vittoria Collona – mysterious, as he was gay.

VITTORIA: 'ows the cealin goin, Mike?
MICHEL A: I bin using the long brush but it's doin' me back in.
VITTORIA: Why don't you arst the Pope fer scaffoldin'?
MICHEL A: Oh ta, I knew these visits 'ere wouldn't be wasted.

Hours. We lie on the beach sunning and smoking, and like true smokers throw our dog ends and matches in the sea.

'Hello, down there.' The Colonel's red face is at the grilled Moorish window, his face looking equally grilled. We must come up, tea is being served. A long refectory table laden with salads and a magnificent bronze samovar. Our every whim is waited on slavishly by the little Italian. 'They're a dying breed,' says Startling Grope. (He was right. The Iti died the day after we left.) The officers are slopping down one Alexander after another and we all repair to the beach again; Captain Clarke in a one-piece suit that was out of

64

date when Captain Webb swam the channel, and the Colonel in a pair of bathing drawers of 'the briefest gist'. He plunges in, comes out, and goes up to bed. Captain Clarke strikes out to sea so far that the current gradually carries him out of sight round the headland. He is not shouting 'help' but just in case we shout 'Goodbye, sir.' He disappears. Should we inform the life-guards? No, there's plenty more like him. Hours later he returned overland via the Villa Fondalillo some three miles away. When the Italian flunkey opened the door, a shagged-out Captain Clarke fell into the house, but at least he had two wet legs and a body to match.

Eventide and we are returning; the RAF boat waits at the mole. The Colonel has organized it perfectly, except for falling in the sea again. 'Homeward bound, eh?' says the Captain, and leads our officers away for drinkypoos. We of the lower order stay on deck with buggerallpoos. Ischia fades into the crepuscular evening and Naples looms. We dock.

'You drive, Terence,' says Colonel S. Singing all the while, we are back at Maddaloni in just over the hour and under the weather. It was a memorable day. Even as I type this, I can see that splendid sunlight on that warm azure sea in a time capsule that will never come again.

Len and I are bedding down for the night. 'He must have drunk ten bottles of wine, two of Strega and two of brandy,' Len said. 'You'll see, when he goes it will be his liver or his bladder.' He was wrong: in 1970 Stanley died of heart failure during an operation for piles. But for piles, Stanley would be alive today, doing ten years for interfering with little boys. One of them could have been me. I speak with experience. You see that evening on our return from Ischia, I drove Stanley back to his billet and he put his hand up my shorts. I thought, this could mean promotion for me, but no, I said 'Look here, sir, fuck off . . . sir.' He is sorry. It will never happen again.

Len falls about laughing. 'Cor, fancy, there's men up the line dying and down here the Colonels are trying to grab yer goolies.' I reminded him it was better than dying. 'Let's face it, would you rather be fucked or killed?'

## Ars Gratia Artist

I have entered an Art Contest, and I win!

*Nude winner of art contest*

The prize is given me by a new man, Major Rodes of the Highland Light Infantry. He too is gay, and has just returned from some daring deed behind the enemy lines, like squeezing partisans' balls under fire. Now he is out of the line as he has developed a hernia (did he use a dark room?) and he is billeted with us awaiting an operation. This has been delayed by Brigadier Henry Woods who is a 'rupture expert' and wants to get the Major the right hospital and the right surgeon. So, I receive my prize from a ruptured major who was a professional artist in Civvy Street! Did he chalk the pavements? He laughs not. My drawing is very good, had I done any artistic training? I told him I'd done a bit in Goldsmith's College. He said never mind her, would I like to do murals? Had I ever done any murals? Yes, I did 'All Coppers are Bastards' outside the Lady Flo' Institute, Deptford, 1936. He shows me a drawing of Hyde Park Corner in high Victorian days. He wants to do an enlargement on the wall of the Officers' Mess. 'There'll be something in it for you,' he says. O K, I'll do it. Murals; mean swines, anything to save buying wallpaper. Evenings I don my denims and start work.

I square off the wall and then draw the enlargements.

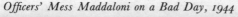

*Officers' Mess Maddaloni on a Bad Day, 1944*

*Military supplies showing liver cripplers, Maddaloni, 1944*

To my delight it comes very easily. It means working late after the Officers' Mess closes, but in lieu I'm given time off in the mornings. I am praised. 'My word, you are talented, Terence,' says Stanley, Sir. 'You play the trumpet and guitar and you can paint. Is there anything you can't do?' Yes, sir, Sheila Frances.

The Colonel is to do a tour of the front lines. Would I like to come too? The front line? Does he think I'm mad? He does. No sir, my days of sitting in an O P trench full of water with 88s air bursting over your head and your bottle bursting underneath are over. 'Goodbye, good luck, God be with you, but not me.'

O2E is womanless, save for tall lovely ATS Captain Thelma Oxnevad, six foot with sparkling blue eyes and certain things . . . We like each other, but alas, she is an officer and a gentleman and I am a gunner, the stuff that gutters are made of.

'No Spike, I can't walk out with you.'

I don't want her to walk out, I want her to walk into my bedroom. No, if Brigadier Henry Woods heard this, she'd be cashiered and I'd be shot. I tell her that's O K with me. I tell her that when we take our clothes off she wouldn't be able to tell the gunner from the Captain! Nay nay nay. When I dance with her, she is three inches taller. I explain that lying down we will both be the same height. Even as I dance with her, I can feel the eyes of other officers on me, jealous with rage. Like Major Rodes, he wants to dance with me. Thelma gives me hope.

'Your lust will soon be allayed Spike, a consignment of virgin ATS are to be posted here.'

Meantime I still try to home in on Sheila Frances. She gives in! Yes, she *will* meet me. She'll never regret it! With me in my Prime and all parts in Grand Prix order. Ah yes, she'll love my Grand Prix. 8 o'clock outside the 604 ATS Company HQ Caserta.

I am there, beautiful, radiating Brasso, Blanco, Bryl-creem and Brio, with all my things revolving at high speed. I am there dead on 8 o'clock, I am also there dead on at half-past eight, I am also dead on there at nine, and I am there dead on again at nine-thirty, and I went on to be dead on at ten o'clock. Where was she, my little darling dirty rotten little tart, letting me and it down! Today I wonder, was I at the right address? Somewhere in the street of Caserta is a grey-haired old lady in a ragged ATS uniform still waiting for it.

I withdraw to the Forces Canteen in the High Street and am found drinking tea, eating a sandwich and finding consolation watching the wobbling bum of the manageress. Next day Major Rodes and his rupture hear of my adventure. 'So your little soldier tart didn't show, eh?' He hands me a drawing.

ATS
QUARTERS

1945

Spiked

Maddaloni
Italy
1944

## Band Biz

We want to expand the band. We would like a string section. There is a fine fiddler, one Corporal Spaldo. At concerts he plays Montés' Czardas. Would he like to play in our band? He shudders. No, not for him the nigger rhythm music. There is a postscript to this tale.

Many years after the war I was in a night club. The cabaret is supplied by a 'Krazy Kaper' Band. I notice a violinist, wearing a large ginger wig and beard, a football jersey, a kilt with a whitewash brush for a sporran, fishnet stockings and high heel shoes. They play 'Does chewing gum leave its flavour on the bedpost over night'. It's Spaldo! I couldn't resist it, I went over and said, 'Changed your mind, eh?'

So my lotus days in the band continued. We were paid three hundred lire a gig, my trumpet solos working out at a penny a time. Our finances were organized by Welfare Officer Major Bloore. He sometimes writes to me from the Cayman Islands.

Now I am *moved* from Filing to the Welfare Office, under the eye of Private Eddie Edwards.

*Pte. E. Edwards*
*Posed with a soft filter,*
*facing Nor' East and*
*lightly oiled*

I am to draw posters for the current films being shown. My first one is Rita Hayworth. No, I'm not doing it right, says Major Rodes, try again. Rita Hayworth I I, no, it's not right. Rita Hayworth I I I, I V, V, V I, V I I, V I I I, no, I just can't get Rita Hayworth right for *West of Pecos*; I can't even get her right for East, North or South of Pecos.

'Sir, I didn't join the army to draw a regiment of Hayworths. I want out!'

'You fool, you little khaki fool,' losing a golden opportunity to become the great artist he could make me. The Major stamps off in a kilt-swinging rage.

'He's very temperamental,' says Eddie.

'I think he's in the change,' I reply. 'And his truss must be upside down.'

## The Aquarium Club

This is to be a new officers' drinking club. The venue is a farmhouse just outside the town.

S. Milligan
Italy 1944
Maddaloni.

My penance is to do more murals. This time sea life. The Major drives me to the site. There are no men on the farm. 'Tutti nella Armata.' At the moment they were all planting cabbages in Sussex; among them Mario and Franco who were to stay on to revolutionize our eating habits with their trattorias. Only the mother and the daughter Maria were left (in Italy all daughters not called mothers are Marias). She is a rough peasant beauty, five foot seven inches, tall for an Italian, and very tall for a dwarf. She has large brown expressive legs and eyes, tousled black hair and brown satin skin. (Arrrghhh!) Her mother, pardon me, looked like a bundle of oily rags ready for sorting. She seemed ever fearful of her daughter being screwed, whereas I wasn't worried at all. They were poor and leasing out a few rooms was salvation to them. She shows us two upstairs rooms. As Maria walked up the stairs, I made a note of her shapely bottom, while the Major made a note of mine. The rooms were being painted light marine blue by defaulters. Poor devils, here they had come to face Hitler, and instead they're stripping and painting walls, just like Hitler did twenty years ago. 'No wonder he went fucking mad,' they said. On the morrow I was to apply my skills; very nice, no filing, and away from the Maddening Thomas Hardy.

## A Red Beard and a Beret

By coincidence a real Royal Academician has joined our happy band. George Lambourne, one of Augustus John's many sons, and the image of him. He brings his talents and a batch of Welfare painters to 'tart up' our drab interiors.

I met him when I attended one of his lectures. He was too good to miss. I made a point of taking him to dinner at Aldo's Café. Talk was of painting. So, I'm doing murals. Did I go to art school? He is a bit puzzled by my scatty way of jumping from one subject to another like Queen Elizabeth the First, but I must have made an impression. Bear witness to mention in his diary.

Fri: 22 Early breakfast. Left Naples 7.30 for Maddaloni. Library painting nearly finished. Partition up book shelves beginning. Lounge YMCA going well. Sgts mess begun (changing scheme). Dinner at mess. Talk with Tubby Clayton (TOC H) and more important with Col. Thompson & Col Harrington re John Hewell as librarians and new man Milligan. attended committee meeting of library. Feeling extremely tired and somewhat out of condition. but mostly tired.

I remember George pouring me a glass of red wine, and feeling the glow of his personality. A man of depth, character, talent and brains. Who were his favourite painters? He reels off a mixture – Giotto, Rubens, Boudin, Van Gogh. What about me?

'What do you like drawing, Spike?'

I told him. 'Pay.'

Talking about Turner's sunsets: 'You never see a sunset like that,' I said. 'No,' said George, 'but don't you wish you did!'

George died a few years ago. The world is a colder place.

## The Murals

I'm there on the plank drawing enlarged fish, octopus, squid, dolphins and crabs; thank God I've never had them as bad. Maria drops in to see how I'm faring; there's a bit of flirting; she brings me figs, oranges, grapes. I ask her if she has a relative in Pompeii. We are repeatedly interrupted by the croaking voice of her mother – 'MARIAAAAAAAAA DOVE VI' – accompanied by sudden rushes into the room. Suspicious, yet disappointed. One arrives at the conclusion that the moment an Italian girl isn't visible to her parents she's screwing.

Their farm was a tumbledown affair, and the farm dog, Neroni, a mongrel, was a sad sight, tethered on a piece of rope that only allowed him three paces, nothing more or less than a hairy burglar alarm. The forecourt was a mess of stabling, two white longhorn oxen, a few bundles of silage, scattered farm tools and a wooden plough (in 1944!), a few chickens and goats, the latter given to the desertification of Italy. Poor Neroni, whenever I approached he would snarl and bark like crazy, but when close to, he cowered and whimpered. I got him a longer piece of rope. I stroked him, something no one had ever done before. He licked my face. I brought him some food which he wolfed down. I often think of him. Those days were among the best I'd ever have. At morning I'd breakfast and then make my way to the farm down a dusty lane. The landscape was not unlike Arles at the time of Van Gogh. I'd work through the mornings. I brought the mother some tea, sugar and tins of bully beef. She wept and kissed my hand. Never mind that, what about a screw with Maria!

By the first week in October I had completed the murals at the Aquarium Club. I arranged to finish mid-morning so I could sneak the rest of the day off. I pack up my pots of paint, wash out the brushes. Tomorrow I will steal another day off when I come to collect them. Goodbye Maria, Momma and Neroni. I walk back by the dusty road and pass a goat flock. A large she-goat is about to deliver. The goat herder, a boy of fourteen, is stroking her and saying 'Piano, piano.' Why did a goat need a piano at this particular time? Finally the little hooves start to protrude. The boy, with consummate skill, takes the heels and pulls the kid clear, then repeats it on the twin, alley opp! The little kids, shiny and shivery, lie still as their mother licks them. In minutes they are standing on jellified legs; seconds later they are at the teat sucking vigorously. It was all miraculous in its way, as moving as a Beethoven Quartet – now that needs a piano!

## Il Bagno

October is still warm, the waters call. At the rear of the
Great Palace at Caserta is a great cascading water course,
Bacino Grande e Caserta.

Caserta - Parco Reale - Bacino Grande e Cascata

The faded illustration I include, as it was bought on this
very day. Ah, those marble water gardens, cascades gush
over Diana of the Chase, poor Atteone being attacked by
hounds. How is he supposed to obtain his romantic ends

Caserta - Parco Reale - Bagno di Atteone

*American Red Cross Cinema and Lamppost*

with gallons of algae-ridden water cascading over him and dogs snapping at his balls?

This green sward where the Bourbons once sported has now been given over to the Allied soldiery and wham bam, it's become a swimming pool. Hundreds of leaping, diving, splashing, plunging, coughing, spitting loonies are churning the waters. NAAFI stalls have mushroomed, lemonade, ice-cream, cakes, tea are all on tap. We have created Jerusalem in Italy's pleasant land. Along with the 02E Cook House staff, I am in there somewhere, witness following photographs.

Tell me what's clever about: 'Who can hold their breath under water longest? – winner gets 20 lire.' Believe me, some of them nearly *died* in the attempt. This was the sort of stuff submariners dreaded, yet here we were doing it for 20 lire! We swam until sunset or death, then repaired to the American Red Cross cinema in the High Street.

It was a Mickey Rooney, Judy Garland film with the 'Hey, why don't we put on a show' crap. What had appeared to be a barn suddenly becomes the Carnegie Hall with six musicians sounding like a hundred and twenty; an unknown milkman, played by José Iturbi, plays Hungarian Rhapsody, tap danced by three hundred girls; Mickey Rooney tap dances, sings, plays the drums, the trombone, the piano, the fridge, the miracle of loaves and fishes, and then, for reasons only known to God, they all start to march towards the camera. Will Gracie appear? No, they all sing God Bless America, F D R and the Chase Manhattan Bank.

What an exciting life we were leading.

## The Prodigal Returns

Stanley Sir is back from the front (how's that?). He's heard that I've finished the Aquarium Club. 'Major Rodes is very pleased.' So he should be, he didn't have to do it. Stanley Sir points to the map of his tour. I was here, here and here. Not at the same time, surely. We were shelled here, and a German plane strafed us here. I told you not to play with those boys up the road.

## 'Wedding Bells are Ringing for Mary but not for Mary and Me' (popular song, circa 1928)

Brigadier Henry Woods is in love! Who is she that will marry this World War I Worrier at the age of 104? Let Milligan tell all.

The story starts in Humphrey Bogart country, North Africa, land of the Bedouin, the Tuareg, the Clap. After the Torch landings, Henry Woods and his gallant band of clerks dash in and seize the offices, to assist the bureaucracy. He hires two sweaty blue-chinned Algerian Arabs and a French colonial girl, Mademoiselle Ding. They had all worked for Admiral Darlan before his assassination. Now they would work for Brigadier Woods before *his* assassination. The trio all speak fluent French and Arabic. When they move to Italy they come to speak to any Italians that spoke Arabic. By now Henry has fallen in love with Mademoiselle Ding! He proposes, she accepts. Soon they usher forth from the portals of St Michael's Maddaloni. A guard of honour, clerks holding pens, form a bridal arch, the bells ring out, and the Honeymoon? Largo Como! There the happy couple dwell in bliss. But what's this? One day Henry arises and what's this? The bird has flown. 'L'oiseau est partie.' Fancy, here in this miserable backwater Maddaloni, the Neasden of Italy, deceit and despair, he has been cuckolded! How? Well, one of the blue-chinned Algerians had a few months back asked for permission to visit his relatives in Paris, people like Laval, Petain, etc., so with all found paid and a khaki handshake, he departs. Could he be the 'other' man? Henry is suspicious. He sends Major Rodes and his hernia (yes, they still haven't found the right doctor) to seek and kill. It is all as exciting as a B movie.

## Algerian Sheik Sweeps Brigadier's Wife From Under Nose of Husband

Major Rodes' search leads him to Paris, and success. There at a table for deux, he finds Mademoiselle Ding and the Arab. Ah, if only the *Sun* could have got the story.

## ENGLISH BRIGADIER MARRIES FRENCH ALGERIAN THIRTY YEARS YOUNGER

'Age makes no difference,' she says.

## STOP PRESS: THIRTY YEARS YOUNGER 'AGE MAKES NO DIFFERENCE' BRIDE MISSING!

Thirty Years Younger French Bride
Caught In Flagrante With
Algerian Arab In Bedford Hotel Paris.

'Age makes no difference,' she says.

## BRIGADIER HAS ARAB'S BALLS CUT OFF

'Age makes no difference,' says Brigadier.

Thus Major Rodes brought his rupture and the sad story back.

# ROME

## October 9

MY DIARY: BAND GIG IN ROME. WHOOPEE!

Rome! The Eternal City! Forever young! Age makes no difference here, unless you're Henry Woods.

We travel by Welfare Charabanc. Early morning the charabanc arrives at Alexander Barracks. We eagerly pack our stuff aboard. Len Prosser is worried about the safety of his bass. In its canvas sack he appears to be smuggling a murdered body aboard. 'The man who invented this instrument never intended it to travel – it's meant for hermits or the transfixed.' Drums. Vic Shewry is coming and going. Percussion seems unending. 'When you two have finished we'd like to bloody well get on,' says Jim Manning and his alto sax. Up and away a hundred and fifty miles to go, so a cigarette and the Union Jack and I settle back. The Allies are driving the Germans back over the Po River. It must be hard on German mothers to receive telegrams:

## Hitlergram No. Sieben

ZER FÜHRER REGRETS TO INFORM YOU YOUR SON HAZ BEEN DROWNED IN ZER PO.

Through ancient Capua, over the Volturno, Sparanise, Teano; all the roads I'd passed through in action. Memories of 19 Battery, the sound of the guns, the shout of fire orders, now all passing into the dreamtime. Through Cassino, and above it the ruined abbey, a monument to Allied stupidity. We rabbit, joke and laugh our way. Come evening we reach our destination. '56 Area Rest Camp Welcomes You'. It's like Belsen with food.

'This is yours,' says a lumpy Corporal, opening the door of a Nissen hut. It is a paradise of wooden beds and blankets!

'So,' says Len Prosser with an expansive gesture, '*this* is Broadway!'

We get comfortable, try the beds for lumps. Q M S Ward is to speak.

He holds up a hand like Custer halting the 7th Cavalry. 'Ye-o-oh.' He reads from a stained paper. 'The first gig is tomorrow, Crusaders Officers' Club, leave here 1900 hours, best battledress.'

We have the evening to ourselves. Ah! The Alexander Club! We walk out in the sunlit wide streets; people here in no way resemble their grotty cousins in Naples. Lots of pretty girls. On the Via X X September we find the Alexander Club. It is a massive modern concrete and glass horror, a sort of Orson Wells of architecture. Inside a milling sea of squaddies, a cacophony of rattling plates, cups, knives, forks and spoons; it sounds like Lyons Corner House going over Niagara Falls. 'Christ!' says Jim Manning. 'Aren't there any bleedin' soldiers at the front?' He's wrong. We join a queue for tea and *all* the soldiers are at the front. It winds back two hundred yards. We look like the Israelites crossing the Red Sea. Tea, buns, fags; fags, buns, tea; buns, tea, fags. Opposite the Alexander is a chrome and glass Italian barber's. Smart glossy-haired white-jacketed Largo Factotums are in attendance. Len and I are grovelled into our foot-operated adjustable chairs, crisp white sheets are tucked around our necks. I had never savoured the delights of an Italian shave, and now he was whisking up the lather like an egg white. I hadn't seen such manual dexterity since Mademoiselle Fifi le

Toof of the Cages, Bombay. With a chamois leather cloth he cleans my skin with an astringent. With fast revolving circles he lathers me with an aromatic soap made from almond oil. It's all too good for me. Honing a razor on a black leather strap, he gently scrapes upwards, the bristles falling in hundreds. He feels for any areas he has missed and plies the blade over them, repeating the whole process twice. It's all done with a marvellous rhythmic precision, the blade so sharp that there is no pulling or tearing of the skin. A glance in the mirror, no shaving soap remains. Now he applies hot towels that he juggles from hand to hand to release the heat. The face is enveloped and the smell of cologne rises with the steam. This done, an ice cold astringent is patted on to the skin. It's taken twenty-five minutes. We have seen a great artist at work. Len has asked his to marry him. My face feels like fine velvet; I am reeking of a cologne that will make a woman rip her clothes off at fifty paces. I must hurry on to the streets before it wears off.

*L./Bdr. L. Prosser and Gunner T. Milligan. After being shaved, they are waiting at the Fountain of the Naiads for a good trouser press.*

*\* this man is now in America somewhere*

What to do? It's only seven of the clock. We look at our
*Soldier's Guide to Rome* —

# CLUBS, RESTAURANTS and
# CANTEENS reserved for Allied Trops

## BRITISH ARMY

NAAFI, *Alexander Club* - C.I.M. building, Via XX Settembre (20)
Y. M. C. A., *Centenary Club* - Piazza Colonna (7)
Y. M. C. A., *Hotel and Club* - Hotel Victoria - 41, Via Marche (18)
C. W. L. *Club and Canteen* for British and Colonial Forces
161, Via Quattro Fontane (13)
.CHRISTIAN SCIENCE SERVICE CENTRE (cnr. Via 4
Fontane and Via Quirinale) (12)
BRITISH AND DOMINION W. O.s AND SITS Restaurant
(Grotte del Piccione - 37, Via della Vite (off C. Umberto) (10)
CHURCH OF SCOTLAND CANTEEN - P.za Foro Traiano (16)
BRITISH O. R.s RESTAURANTS for day leave personnel.
Admission by ticket only:
RISTORANTE VALIANI, main riwy. station building, (21)
and RISTORANTE DAL BOLOGNESE - Piazza del Po-
polo (top of Corso Umberto). (3)
X YEWISH SOLDIERS' CLUB - 37, Piazza Poli, Via del Tri-
tone. Synagogue (11)
WESLEY HOUSE - 5, Via XX Settembre (20)
INDIAN CLUB, Ristorante Rosetta - 22, Via Giustiniani
(cnr. of the Pantheon Square) (4)
SPRINGBOK CLUB for UDF and Rhodesian ORs, - 3 Via
Romagna (18)
BILLIARD SALOON - 12, Via Francesco Crispi (opposite
tunnel in via del Tritone) (10)
AFC AUSTRALIAN CLUB - 18, Corso Vittorio Emanuele.
Near Piazza Venezia (8)
ART EXHIBITION ROOMS (Via Nazionale;. Exhibition of
water colour paintings, organised by British Army Sec-
tion of Rome Arts Club (15)

## OFFICERS' CLUB and RESTAURANTS

Y. M. C. A. *Officiers Club* - 82, Largo Brancaccio 3mins.
from S. M. Maggiore (23)
NIRVANETTA CLUB - 25, Via dei Maroniti, Largo Tritone (11)
CRUSADER CLUB (opposite Grand Hotel). Lunch, tea and
dinner, billiards, dancing nightly) (21)
COLEBRI CLUB - 87, Via Boncompagni (19)
CASINA VALADIER - Pincio Gdns., near Piazza del Popolo (24)

The numbers between ( ) are those by wich every club or restaurant is indicated on the map.

'That one looks interesting, Len.' I say, pointing out the Yewish Soldiers' Club. So there *are* such people as Yews; they must come from Yewrusaleum. We opt for the Super Cinema in the Via Depretis. The film is *Sweet Rosie O'Grady*, starring Betty Grable's legs, and occasionally her. The hero, whose name escapes me, was John Payne; a fitting name for a pain in the arse. It's San Francisco, but recently vacated by Jeanette MacDonald and Clarke Gable, John Payne is a struggling pianist. He's also having a struggle acting. He falls in love with Betty Grable's legs, she falls in love with his bad acting, but the boss of the bar loves her legs more. Payne writes 'My heart tells Me'; he tells her, 'You sing it baby, it'll be a hit, you'll see.' The boss says, 'She ain't singin' no trashy song like that, dis goil I'm savin' fer Opera.' Payne hits the boss, the boss hits Payne, they hit each other, they break, there is the traditional breaking of the matchstick chair over the hero, who floors the boss. 'You're fired,' he snarls. 'Huh, fired, I'll quit.' (If only he would.) Payne goes to New York. Diamond Jim Brady hires him on to Broadway; he's in the pit conducting on the big night; Joan Blondell and her tits are going to sing 'My heart tells me' and make him famous. But she faints. Who's going to save the show? Outside in the snow, a ragged unshaven figure appears: it's Betty Grable. She hears the introduction . . . The End. Money back please. So to bed.


## The Gig

We spent the morning lazing. I cleaned my trumpet. In the afternoon band practice, listened to by crowds of soldiers. Comes evening. I couldn't believe it. Little old me from Brockley, in Rome! Back home I'd never got further than Hernia Bay. The dance is at the Crusader Club. Wow! A huge marble hotel, an officer's dream palace.

Colonel Philip Slessor greets us. 'Who's in charge?' he asks.

'You are,' we say.

Tall and saturnine, Slessor was later to become a BBC

announcer. He started practising right away by announcing that we were to follow him.

The ballroom is magnificent, the stage a mass of red velvet and gold embroidery; it was an 'embarrass de choix de richesses'. Slessor makes another announcement. 'There's a room for you all to change in.' We haven't anything to change into except Mr Jekyll.

'What? You're not going to play like that?' Haven't we any mess dress? No, there's another fine mess dress we haven't got into. I told him we sounded exactly the same in battle-dress as we did in mess dress.

'Huh,' he announces.

The band room is a munificence of coleslaw, the table is groaning with every sandwich possible, even a few impossible ones. Wine? Gallons. A line of bottles without labels. We tasted it, found it tasted like unlabelled wine.

Slessor is announcing again: 'We start in ten minutes, lads.' We set up behind the brocade curtains, give him the nod, and he announces: 'Ladies and Gentlemen, we have great pleasure in announcing the Band of the Officers of the Second Echelon under their conductor Sergeant Stand (yes, Stand) Britton. Take your partners for the first Waltz.' The curtains draw back as we swing into 'Song of India'. The floor is soon crammed with dancers, most of the ladies Italian, all desperate for food, fags and soap. It's hard to believe that the beautiful Contessa, dancing with the cross-eyed Hindu colonel, is doing it for three bars of chocolate.

I was blowing great that night. When I stood up to take a chorus it was for one of two reasons: a) Egomania or b) Piles.

The interval, and Colonel Slessor announces that he's 'Very pleased with us'. He then announces he is leaving the room.

Throughout the evening he announced every dance, the names of the tunes, the winners of the spot prize, even 'The trumpet solos were by Gunner Millington.' He really was ready for the 9 o'clock news. Finally 'The last waltz, please.' 'God Save the King', then we moved in on the scoff. It had been a great evening of dancing and announcing; we had

*Colonel Philip Slessor showing an officer the correct dress and stance for announcing*

seen lots of pretty birds but hadn't pulled any, so, as Jim Manning said, 'We'll 'ave ter pull ourselves.'

## The Days

The days of that week were spent visiting every tourist trap available, the Vatican, the Fountains of Rome, the Capitol, the Karzi, during which time I nearly scored.

We have one night off and I go solo walkabout. I'm hovering near the Therme de Caracalla when I hear a sweet female voice laced with sandpaper – there were no words as such – but she is bearing down on me as though I'm an old friend. A Junoesque thirty-five-year-old in black, and wearing an Ascot hat, she grabs my hand and says how good it is to see me again.

'Come sta?'

Oh, I'm very 'sta'. It's all a ploy to avoid the suspicion of being on the game. I like this game, but I want game, set and match. She is desperate, she's short of money and at her wit's end. My type.

She is respectable, she's not on the game, but she's desperate. So am I, I tell her. She says we must retire to a café. She needs a coffee and brandy as she is 'faint', all twelve stone of her. So there we are in the café; she tells me she is married, that her husband is in the Reggimento Aeronautica, though he hasn't been sending her any money. But beware, he is 'molto geloso' and she shows me his photo. He looks like two Al Capones stuffed into a uniform. She thinks he's a prisoner of war 'somewhere'. I hope it's Siberia. Can Gunner Milligan take her to dinner tomorrow? No he can't, he's playing in the band. Oh, so I'm a musician! How romantico! The next night then, yes. I know the Sunday is free. Can I bring her some chocolate, soap, cigarettes, sweets, in fact the entire stores of the Allied 5th Army. There is a promise of female favours in her eyes. Yes I will etc. I tell the boys. They go green with envy, some go yellow and grey.

'Wot's she like?' says Private Manning, lying on his bed looking at the ceiling, imagining it's him. I say she likes the contents of warehouses. I say she's a mixture of Rita Hayworth, Betty Grable and Mae West. I'll make the buggers suffer.

## Romance Two

We meet at the café. She's gone ahead and put two cognacs on my bill. Have I got the goodies? I hand her my meagre parcel, apologizing for omitting the leg of venison and side of beef. She must examine the contents and check these against her list. We must take a horse-drawn carriage, it will be less conspicuous. So we drive down the Corso Umberto while she checks the parcel. Mama mia! Only chocolate, cigarettes and jam? I apologize. Never mind, she knows a 'cosy little' trattoria. This is called La Tantolina and it's disguised as a four-star hotel. I can't believe the swish interior, black velvet and gold cutlery, all tables arranged in private nooks, with lights from chandeliers that look like flying saucers. A trio are playing 'Lae thar piss tub darn bab'. We are seated under the stern gaze of the Maître. 'Hello mate,' I say. He hands me the menu like a summons. One look and I realize I'm hurtling to financial oblivion. Just the soup needs a bank loan. What will madame have? She will have all Milligan's savings, post-war gratuities and his collection of underwear.

'Oh che mangiare,' she says in ecstasy. Why oh why isn't Gunner Milligan eating, why is he only sipping water and not drinking the luscious vintage Masi? I tell her it's my delayed Easter fast. 'Che poverino,' she coos, munching Pollo Romana. I watch her clock up seventeen thousand lire; I have eighteen, I just make it. I give the waiter a ten lire tip, which he throws in the rubbish bin. What now? Revenge in bed. No, she must fly, her mother is ill. She borrows my last 1000 lire, 'Taxi!'

I never saw her again. That night, starving and skint, I could be found diving for coins in the Trevi Fountain. The lads; I lied to them, yes! I'd had it away again and again and again! I couldn't stop her! She said she'd leave her husband and join me in England. I failed to add, in a debtors' prison. Yes, lads, it was some night, now can someone lend me a bar of soap and a fag?

Our final gig is at the Nirvenetta Club, Via de Monoriti; after that we all found our way to the G I Swing Club on the Via Vittoria Collona, a below-ground joint with seepage from the Tiber and an Iti 'swing band' that sounds like seepage from the Tiber – yes, it's 'Lae thar piss tub darn bab'. We don't get a dance – everyone has brought their own bird. Under Mussolini, jazz has been forbidden. This must have been the band that caused it. We ask them if we can sit in; they grudgingly agree. Soon we've wiped them out, we have the place jumping. G Is are appreciative: 'Great! Man, you should have come sooner,' they say. We know. We get free drinks and the Italian musicians sit and glower at our success. First we bomb Monte Casssino and now this.

## Back to Base

On the morrow we drive back to Maddaloni. We arrive in the early evening. During our absence, the old dance hall has been renovated by George Lambourne and his merry painters and looks great. Now we have a stage and an orchestra pit, lighting board, paint frame, the lot. We are forewarned by BQMS Drew Taylor, a khaki Florenz Ziegfeld, that a concert is to be given for the Grand Opening. Have we any contributions? I said mine were in the stomach of a bird in Rome. Can we do a small swing spot? Yes, has he a gallows?

*Gratuitous Space*

Alick Adams reports:

A leading feature of the show was the O2E Dance Band, especially a spot in the second half when, as the programme states, Spike Milligan & the Rythm Section were featured.

I recall that the show was under the patronage of one Brigadier Woods, Deputy Adjutant General, or DAG for short. This proved significant for the aforementioned Spike had written a special number for the concert, 'Doodle With DAG'. 'Doodle' being a euphemism which was in popular use in the Other Ranks Bar at the time. The trumpet solo was of course executed from the horizontal position, the instrumentalist's embouchure being very prominent from this angle.

C M F

Architect: Lt. F. W. SAUNDERS, R.E.     Decoration: GEORGE LAMBOURNE (Army Welfare Services)

# Souvenir Programme

*to commemorate the opening of the*

## O2E CONCERT HALL

on

*Saturday 4th November*

and

*Monday 6th November, 1944*

at 20.15 hrs.

# "STAND BY FOR TELEVISION". A Radio Burlesque

## AN ALL-ECHELON SHOW

This entertainment, as its title implies is a radio burlesque. Sit yourself down in your favourite armchair — let your imagination run riot with you and let it take you back to your own fireside. Your imaginary television set will let you see and hear some of the technicalities of Broadcasting, which, it is our intention to show, may not always be what you think they are.

### The Day's Programme

1. OVER TO THE ANNOUNCER . . . . Time Signal

2. THE "NEWS" . . . . Read to you by JAMES BILLINGTON

3. "UP IN THE MORNING EARLY" . . Instructor ARTHUR BARKER
   (Morning Exercises) . . . . At the Piano HENSON MAW

4. INTERLUDE OF RECORDED MUSIC

5. PART SONGS . . . . ObE MALE VOICE CHOIR

   Including "Bill Song"         Conductor:
     "Drink to Me Only"     FRED WILDERSPIN
     "Annie Laurie"        At the Piano:
     "The Old Woman"     HENSON MAW
     "Gendarme's Song"

            RELAYED FROM THE STUDIO

6. "IN YOUR GARDEN" . . . . Gardening Hints by BOB AUSTIN
   (With apologies to Mr. Middleton)

7. FAT STOCK PRICES FOR FARMERS . read by JAMES BILLINGTON

8. DRAMATIS PERSONNÆ

   Two Poems . . . . . . . . . . ANDREW ALLEN
     (a) "KUBLA KHAN" . . . . by S. T. Coleridge
     (b) "ARABIA" . . . . by Walter De La Mare

           EXTRACT FROM "HAMLET"

   OPHELIA . . . . . . . . . RUTH CONTI
   HAMLET . . . . . . . . . LIONEL HAMILTON

9. LUCKY DIP . . . . . . . A Record at Random

10. VARIETY HALF-HOUR
               Featuring :
   (i) BARKER AND WARD and "MRS. WARD" in a Domestic Dispute
   (ii) SPIKE MILLIGAN AND THE RHYTHM SECTION
   (iii) "THE GREAT ILLUSIONISTS" Featuring: LEN ROLLS and JACK UREN
   (iv) SONGS – HARRY SHEARER (Tenor)
   (v) "DISORDERLY ROOM"

         Scene: Any Coy. Office in OrE

              Cast :
   CHARLIE WARD . . . . . . O.C.
   ARTHUR BARKER . . . . . Coy. Sgt/Major
   LEN ROLLS . . . . . . . . Prisoner
   JACK UREN

11. "SIGNATURE TUNE MEMORIES" . . . . Henson Maw
        (At the Theatre Organ)

12. NEWS FLASHES

13. DANCE MUSIC . . . . . . . ObE Dance Band

14. CLOSING DOWN
             Announcer
           Greenwich Time Signal

              THE KING

We all worked very hard to get the show together and we opened to an enthusiastic reception. I did a mad musical spot called The Ablution Blues, with a pair of pyjama trousers tied to my trumpet that I kept dipping into a bucket of soapy water, then swinging round and drenching the audience. *I* thought it was very funny, I did, I thought it was *very* funny. Thanks to hard work the act was a smash flop. The reception was like the one Judas got at the last supper.

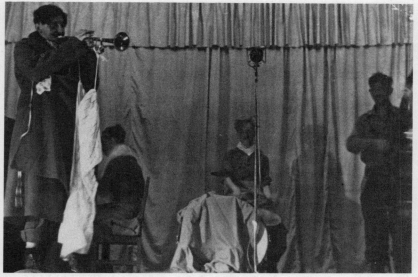

*The Ablution Blues – an overwhelming flop.*
Piano: *Stan Britton;* Drums: *Vic Shewry;* Bass: *Len Prosser*
*Why should I take all the blame?*

The evening concluded with the band playing prior to 'closedown' (see programme). Finally there was a speech on the new stage by the Brigadier, who said all the right things: 'I would like to thank . . . grateful to . . . hard work . . . made it possible . . . not forgetting . . . with the help of . . . debt of gratitude . . . and of course . . . without whose help

... bearing in mind ... last but not least ... has anyone seen Mademoiselle Ding?'

Let's see what George Lambourne thought about it: 'Back to Maddaloni to 02E Concert (opening ceremony). Brigadier Woods in opening speech said a lot of flattering and charming things about me which I did not hear! *I thought the concert very bad.*'

## Religious Interlude

My days of sleeping on O branch office floor were over. I had found a windowless little room up a flight of stairs adjacent to the C of E chapel room at Alexander Barracks. I ask the Rev. Sergeant Beaton if I could sleep in it. Yes, but nothing else, remember! The chapel is next door and there's early services. OK, I move in, and am immediately seized upon to help. Sunday, the 'pumper' for the organ hasn't shown, can I? There, on my knees I am gainfully employed by the Lord. The handle *should* be lowered and raised with an air of delicacy, but Gunner Milligan is a jazz pumper, with a beat-me-daddy-eight-to-the-bar. There is a sickening 'CRACK', I am left with the shaft, and the only way to keep the music going is to activate the remaining four-inch stump. Panicky I pump gallantly, but just can't get enough air into the bellows. The organ fades, and wheezes back to life as the lunatic Gunner tries to keep it operating. No good, it's starting to sound like a bagpipe chanter groaning into life. The congregation are in disarray. Exhausted, I jack it in, the organ 'expires' with a long groan and 'Fissshhhhhh' as the last wind escapes.

Jesus said, 'Through suffering thou shalt come to me.' Well, I was nearly there.

After our weekly Saturday night dance, I would like to hang back and play the piano. I had the illusion that a concerto would come. I was really Cornel Wilde as Chopin. As the climax of the Finale Grandioso con Woodbines, a magnificent ATS Private in a transparent cheesecloth vest would appear and unroll a mattress: 'Come Chopin, forget your silly old Nocturnes – have something else.'

On one such evening, someone does approach. It's a Yewish sergeant who wants to say how much he has enjoyed my trumpet playing. He's just joined the unit and is also keen on show business.

Well, it was the start of a friendship. I let him move into my billet because I thought he had money.

*Sgt. Steve Lewis*
*A Yewish soldier taken*
*in colour because he had*
*money (N.B. due to the*
*publishers' lack of money,*
*it's black and white*
*after all.)*

Help. A giant Yewish bedroll appeared, followed by a Yewish Brigade kitbag, table, chair, tea chest, camouflaged Minorah, and a secondhand copy of the Talmud. He then proceeded to erect the most complicated Heath Robinson network of strings, pulleys, hooks, weights and counter-weights. He wanted to be able to switch lights on and off, raise or lower them, drop his mosquito net, manoeuvre his mess tins and mug near or far, boil a kettle, make tea, toast

99

bread, and open Tower Bridge, all without moving from his bed. I asked him, was he training to be a cripple? He had enough food by his bed to outlast an Atomic War and still open a shop in Golder's Green. If he had been at Masada it would never have fallen; he would have sold it to the Romans. I pointed out that his wasn't the only persecuted race. There were the Irish.

'Spike, the Irish got off light.'

'We took as much stick as you did.'

'Listen, we Jews have been persecuted since Egyptian times.'

I told him I had never read the *Egyptian Times*.

'All you suffered from was a shortage of spuds.'

'Steve, in 1680, there were eleven million Irish. Now there's only two. We lost nine million.'

'Nine million. Oh what a terrible accountant.'

'Don't joke, they were starved, killed, deported or emigrated.'

He laughed. 'You *sure* they weren't Jewish?'

We had unending arguments. 'The Irish? What did they ever have? We had Einstein, Disraeli, Pissarro, Freud. What have the Irish got? Pissed!'

'We got the Pope and Jack Doyle.'

'Jack Doyle the boxer? He's useless!'

'Yes, but we got him.'

'And there's never been an Irish Pope. How come?'

'It's the fare.'

In the shower Steve noticed I'd been circumcised. 'Why?' I didn't know. 'To make it lighter? You know, Milligan, if Jerry took you prisoner, that could have got you into a concentration camp.' It was really something when your prick could get you sent to a concentration camp. 'Believe me, Spike,' says the Yew, 'anyone that sends someone to a concentration camp is a prick.' Amen.

This was the beginning of an ongoing Judaeo-Christian hilarity. When I heard his footsteps on the stairs, I'd call, 'Is that the Yew?' I could hear his stifled giggles.

'Listen Milligan,' he'd say. 'Believe me, the Irish are famous for *nothing*.' And so to Christmas.

Yes, Christmas, bloody Christmas. We decided to do our shopping in Naughty Naples. All up the Via Roma urchins are grabbing us and singing, 'Lae thar piss tub darn bab'. Why in the land of opera do they descend to this crap? If the reverse were to apply in London, little Cockney kids would be singing '*La Donna e Mobile*' as they begged. We make our Christmas purchases and retire to the Royal Palace, NAAFI, where, God help us, we are assailed by God bless her and keep her . . . away from us . . . Gracie Fields. She'd had a bad press at the beginning of the war about living in America, leaving poor Vera Lynn and Ann Shelton to face the bombs. Now she was making up for it. Every day she'd leave her Capri home and bear down on unsuspecting soldiers. 'Ow do lads.' Then, without warning, sing 'Red Sails in the Sunset'.

*A look-out on the Royal Palace* NAAFI *roof, watching for signs of Gracie Fields's boat*

After a while the lads had had enough of 'Ow do lads' and 'Sall-eeee' and the sight of her looming up the stairs would start a stampede out the back, with cries of 'Christ! Here she comes again.' Nothing personal against the dear lady, who had a big heart and an enlarged liver, but she did overdo the 'Eee ba gum, 'ave a cup o' tea lads.'

Sometimes you wouldn't know she was in, until from a distant table, you'd hear 'It's the biggest Aspidistra in the World'. To get rid of her we directed her to a table of Goumiers (Rapists by appointment to the Allies) by telling her they were Gurkhas. 'Sallyyyyyyy, Salleeeee,' she sang at the baffled Moroccans. They didn't even try to rape her.

## December

It's cold, cold, cold. You can strike matches on 'em. My family have had a photo taken that sends a chill of horror through me. Were they dead or stuffed? My brother has the sneer of a high-born Sioux Chief, my mother has had a bag of flour thrown at her face, and my father looks as though he's just been asked to leave for an indiscretion.

A Christmas card from my mother gives my brother second billing, and poor father! Dad is spelt with a small d. Is he getting shorter? There are no traditional Christmas cards in Italy, so I send those available.

For my father I did a funny drawing of a man with a revolving wig. You see, my father wore one. His fear was that any gale over force three lifted the front and transferred it to the back. People wondered why he wore his hat in the Karzi.

## O2E Christmas Arrangements

The Welfare Department had made a Christmas tree that stood by the concert stage. A wonderful effort dressed in crepe paper, cotton-wool balls and little candles. Pity about the fire.

We are putting up snow scenes with make-do commodities.

*My brother, mother and father, Desmond, Florence and Leo Milligan*

*A Christmas card from my parents in Brentwood, posted October 10 1944*

Buon Natale

*To my parents*

*To my brother*

We ask the Sick Bay for six rolls of cotton wool and are told that no one can be hurt that bad and live. I pack my presents. Mother has a small glass bubble enclosing Virgin Mary and Child; a good shake and they are obscured in a snow-storm, and death by hypothermia. Father will have his favourite King Edward cigars, but brother Desmond? What do you send a squaddie in the front line? Of course, a slit trench. No, I send him a sandbag, and, just in case he doesn't laugh, a box of preserved fruit.

## Christmas Eve

Pouring, ice-cold rain. Steve and I are sitting in the festively decorated canteen. We feel seasonal but would rather feel an ATS. We are taking a little wine for our stomachs' sake, also for our liver, spleen and giblets. The strains of Sergeant Wilderspin and his O2E choir are approaching. They enter, singing 'God Rest Ye Merry, Gentlemen' and sneezing. They are collecting for ye Army Benevolent Fund and are soaked to ye skin. At eight o'clock we all file into the concert hall to see the Nativity Play. It's very good, except the dialects jarred. An Angel of the Lord: 'Thar goes t'Bethlehem, sither,' and his sidekick answers, 'Weail off tae sae him right awa.' It didn't detract from the finale around the manger, the choir singing 'Adeste, fideles'. In that moment all minds were back home by the fire, screwing on the rug. Numerous curtain calls, the Brigadier makes a speech ' . . . a great deal of effort . . . a special debt of gratitude . . . not forgetting . . . screwing on the rug . . . also like to thank . . . A Merry Christmas to all our readers . . . has anyone seen Mademoiselle Ding?'

Stop the festivities! The Germans have broken our lines in the Ardennes, all our washing is in the mud! Yet another it's-going-to-be-over-by-Christmas-promise gone. Still, it could be worse. Like poor old Charlie Chaplin who was in a paternity suit – unfortunately it fits him.

◆Steve Lewis looks up from his newspaper, stunned! How

can this happen? Will Hitler win after all? Should he telegraph his wife and say, 'Sell the stock, only take cash.' Stay
cool. Help is coming. Is it John Wayne? No, it's Sheriff
Bernard Law Montgomery. He is going to 'tidy up' the
battle, which ends with him claiming he's won it, and he will
shortly rise again from the dead. Eisenhower is furious. He
threatens to cut Monty's supply of armoured jockstraps and
Blue Unction. Monty apologizes: 'Sorry etc., etc. You're
superior by far, Monty.'

Christmas came and went with all the trimmings, tinned
turkey, stuffing, Christmas Pud, all served to us by drunken
Sergeants. Now we were all sitting round waiting for 1945.
It had been a good year for me. I was alive.

## January 1945

Cold and rain.


Letter from home.


Very quiet month.


Then, on 23 February 1945, this drastic message was flashed
to the world from the pages of *Valjean*, the O2E house
magazine.

### Trumpeter.

Is there no stylish trumpeter in the ranks of
the Echelon ?  At present the O2E Dance Orchestra is handicapped to a certain extent by the
lack of one of these only too rare musicians.
Ex-trumpeter "Spike" Milligan, who has now
gone on to the production line, had to hang up
his trumpet on medical grounds, so if there is
a trumpeter in our midst please contact SQMS
Ward of R/O.

Milligan has hung up his trumpet! A grateful nation gave thanks!

It started with pains in my chest. I knew I had piles, but they had never reached this far up before. The Medical Officer made me strip.

'How long has it been like that?' he said.

'That's as long as it's ever been,' I replied.

He ran his stethoscope over my magnificent nine-stone body. 'Yes,' he concluded, 'you've definitely got pains in your chest. I can hear them quite clearly.'

'What do you think it is, sir?'

'It could be anything.'

Anything? A broken leg? Zeppelin Fever? Cow Pox? La Grippe? Lurgi?

'You play that wretched darkie music on your bugle, don't you?'

'Yes, sir.'

*The band without me. As you can see, they don't sound half as good*

'You must give it up.'

'Why?'

'I hate it.' He goes on to say, 'It's straining your heart.'

Bloody idiot. It's 1985, I'm a hundred and nine, and I'm still playing the trumpet. He's dead. At the time I stupidly believed him and packed up playing.

The first Saturday Music Hall of the New Year was a split bill. The first half Variety, the second half, a play *Men in Shadow*. It was seeing the latter that prompted me to do a lunatic version of our own. We timed it to go on the very night after the play finished, using all the original costumes and scenery.

### Men in Gitis.

Tomorrow the chief attraction at the Concert Hall will be the super, skin-creeping, spine-tingling production "Men in Gitis". In it are the craziest crowd of local talent that one could imagine. Spim Bolligan, the indefatiguable introducer of this new type of show, describes it as "colossal".

I wrote the script with Steve Lewis and Len Prosser. It was total lunacy, starting the play before the audience came in; several of the actors outside the hall doing the first act to the queue; the curtain going up and down throughout the play; the orchestra coming into the pit calling out 'Bread . . . give us bread,' then proceeding to tune up every ten minutes. Bodies were hauled up to the ceiling by their ankles asking for a reduction in rent; people came through trap doors, and all the while a crowd of soldiers done up as Hitler tried to get a grand piano across the stage, and then back again. It ended with the projection of the Gaumont British news all over us, with the music up loud, while the band played 'God Save the King' at speed. As the audience left we leapt down among them with begging bowls, asking for money, and shouted insults after them into the night. How were we received? See below.

ENTERTAINMENTS—*contd. from Page 1.*

## ENTERTAINMENTS—*contd. from Page 1.*

### Music Hall

Last Saturday's Musical Hall was one of the best ever presented. The highspot was undoubtedly "Men in Gitis" – a satirical sequel to "Men in Shadow". This type of show is either liked or hated, and quite a few did not care for it at all, but the majority of people present gave the distinguished performers a really good ovation. "Spike" Milligan was at his craziest and the show was a cross beween "Itma" and "Hellzapoppin".

The entry of Major Bloor, Major New and the RSM added to the enjoyment of this burlesque which culminated in the "Mass Postings" poster being exhibited.

I love that 'good ovation' as against a bad one, however it wasn't bad for lunatics. Spurred by success, like vultures we prepared to wreck the next play. This was . . .

### Future Attractions

Tonight and tomorrow there is the well advertised "White Cargo" showing in the Concert Hall. This play, which some may remember seeing in pre-war days, has a first class story running throughout and should definitely not be missed.

The innocent actor-manager putting it on was Lt. Hector Ross. No sooner was *White Cargo* over than *Black Baggage* was on its way. With maniacal relish we went on to destroy the play piecemeal. The best part of it was that we had persuaded Hector Ross to keep appearing and saying lines from the original show, then bursting into tears and exiting. It was uproarious fun. I didn't know it, but I was taking my first steps towards writing the Goon Show. For this I have to thank Hitler, without whose war it would never have happened.

SOMEWHERE IN THE GULAG ARCHIPELAGO 1984 NINETY-YEAR-OLD HITLER IS SHOVELLING SHIT AND SALT.

HITLER: Hear zat? You must let me be free. I am zer inventor of zer Coon Show. Ven zer Queen hears zis she will giff me zer O B E and ein free Corgi.

Black Baggage *in progress. X marks Spike*

## Romance Three

To brighten up our winter gloom, we have been sent some thirty ATS ladies. Scrotum Agitators. No longer shackled by the band, I could stay on the dance floor, dazzling them with my masterful command of the Waltz, which I had perfected ever since I learned to count up to three. Among this new clutch of steaming females are two little darlings, Rosetta Page and 'Candy' Withers. I have my eyes on them, and hope to get my hands on later. Stage one: the chat-up-in-the-dance. Rosetta is a great dancer. Oh she's from Glasgow? How interesting! Isn't that where Harry Lauder appeared? I didn't get far with Rosetta. Candy. Good evening, do you come here often? Only during wars. Ha ha. Why had I given up playing the trumpet? I daren't tell her it was a suspected coronary. I mean, no respectable ATS wants to be found under a dead gunner. No! I wanted to concentrate on Buddhism. Oh really? Yes, I'd always been into Buddhism. It explored the upper ventricles. The ventricles? Yes. I couldn't go into that now, but would she like to come outside, strip naked, and see what happened? No? Did I hear right? Did she say No to a handsome waltzing 1-2-3 gunner Milligan? Yes. Oh fuck! She's going out with a Sergeant, but she does 'like me'. I said could I see her in between? In between what? Sheets. Don't be silly. OK, can I see her in between Sergeants? Sergeants? She's only going out with one. Good – could I see her in between him? OK, Sunday. Sunday we'll go to Caserta Palace. We'll walk through the gardens then I'll try and screw her; then we'll have tea at the Palace NAAFI and I'll try and screw her; we will then go to the cinema, where certain delights will accompany the Clark Gables! A Sunday came . . . and went. I tell you folks, holding hands is no substitute. I returned to my bedroom bent double with strictures from the waist down. Steve is up late reading the *Jewish Chronicle*. He's deep into an article about Hitler never having been seen in the nude, but I'm not interested in nude Hitlers, I want nude Candy. How could I bend her to my will? Then the words of my friendly district visiting rapist camed to me. The hot weather! Of course! Heat made women more available, hence the invention of Central Heating. So I planned it all. Next time I met the little darling I'd take her to a warm room, close the windows, turn up the heating, make her drink boiling Horlicks then massage her with Sloane's Linament. If that failed I'd set fire to her, then leap on. I kept sending her billets-doux and my measurements.

## The Printed Word in Maddaloni

Our Librarian, Corporal John Hewitt, tried to foster the written word. Till he arrived our library had no one in charge of our book. He put it to rights by procuring numerous volumes. 'This,' he said, holding up a ragged book with covers hanging like limp wings, 'this is the Bible of the masses.' *No Orchids for Miss Blandish*. He points to the drool stains. I'm above this, I have borrowed Darwin's *Origin of the Species*, which my father had said was 'Rubbish'. *He* was the origin of the species. Hewitt wants to know why I've had Dante's *Divine Comedy* for two months. I daren't tell him it's a counter-weight on Lewis's mosquito net. 'Twas Hewitt,

## LONDON

Oh London, none sufficiently can praise
The courage flowering 'mid your smoke maze
Of Limehouse alleys and suburban streets;
From every home unfailing humour beats
Each newer outrage with a newer jest,
And death has never claimed but second best.
This deathless spirit freed from shattered bones
Scarce sheds a tear above your broken stones
Scarce pauses for a moment longer than
It takes to snap the slender life of man,
'Ere taking stand within another heart,
Doubling the measure of its counter-smart
Until today your limitless reserve
Of courage, breaks the Nazis' vaunted nerve.

W. J. O'Leary, Pte.

himself a poet (silly to be not yourself and a poet) who introduced poetry contests, which he lived to regret.

'That was the winner,' he said sobbing on my shoulder. 'You should have seen the bad ones,' he lamented.

## Furlough

Yes. 'We've been furloughed,' said Steve, holding up Part Two Orders. Why had we been furloughed? In appreciation of our *Men in gitis* efforts. One whole week in the Capital again. We are away next morning, Sgt. Steve Lewis, Private Eddie Edwards and Gunner S. Milligan. It looked like an old joke. 'There was this Englishman, this Irishman and this man of the Hebrew persuasion and they were all in the Army, and then one day, ha ha ha, they were all given leave to Rome, ha ha ha.' Once again it's the 56 Area Rest Camp. Steve, being senior, signs us in. 'You realize I've signed for you bastards. For God's sake please avoid the following: rape, murder, arson, little boys, gefilte fish, Mlle Ding.' We queued for a dinner of Irish stew, sponge roll and custard.

*Steve Lewis, Eddie Edwards and Spike Milligan There was an Englishman, an Irishman and a Jew . . .*

Tired after a hard day's travel, we ate it, then wrote off for compensation. The Yew, Lewis, has bagged the favoured upper bunk. 'It's the English class system,' he explains. 'If a wild beast gets in it eats the lower class first, allowing the upper class to survive and re-let the bed for the next victim.' Next morning, early hot showers, singing, towel flicking on the bums etc., then breakfast of sausage, bacon, bread and jam, and we are like giants refreshed. We go on the town.

We are accosted outside a souvenir shop. 'Hey Joe,' says an Iti tout. I tell him my name is not Joe, but Terence Alan Milligan and have a care. Do I want a picture? 'Your-a-face-a-painted in five-a-minutes flat.' Do I want a flat face? O K-o. I must have had a face like a po – he has named me Jerry.

The Colosseum is to Rome what the Eiffel Tower is to Paris but less rusty. 'That's where they threw the Christians to the lions,' says Eddie. No Jews? 'No, the lions weren't kosher.' We eat gelati at a café; visit the Forum. 'Not much of it left,' says Eddie. I tell him that the Forum was destroyed by Vandals. 'I know, they did in our local phone box,' he said.

The Parthenon; two thousand years old and still intact! – the Barbara Cartland of Architecture. Within are the tombs of the Kings and Queens of Italy and there, immured in marble, is Michelangelo. Steve is very impressed. 'What did he die of?' I tell him: 'He fell off the scaffolding.' He is trying to translate the plaques.

'Pity they're in Latin.'

'Why?'

'It's a dead language.'

'Well they *are* all dead.'

I couldn't believe it! Me from Brockley standing where Agrippa stood; it was as absurd as finding Agrippa queuing for fish in Catford. Steve is telling me he has cracked it. 'Agrippa,' he says, laughing at the terrible pun. 'Agrippa is . . . Latin for hair grips.' I thought I heard a groan from the tomb of Michelangelo.

Outside we turn into the Corso Umberto and witness the

great cat colony. An old Italian lady is feeding them (as is the Roman custom). In answer to my query she says the cats have been here 'Lontano fa', so I tell my two chums, 'They've been here since lontano fa.' Steve says, 'That's strange – they miaow in English.'

The Fontana de Trevi and its songs in water: it cascades, gushes, ripples, drips, laughs, squirts. It is magnificent.

I toss the traditional coin in. 'What did you wish?' says Steve. I explain certain things about Candy and he is well pleased. Eddie throws his coin in; he won't say what, but if it was to retire and live in Southampton and go grey, it's been granted. Steve screws up his Jewish soul and throws in a low-denomination coin. What does he wish? He wishes he hadn't thrown it in. We hold back as he starts to strip.

Food. A small restaurant, 'La Bolla' in the Via Flamania, a four-star place – you can see them through a hole in the roof. Here we are in the land of pasta, and I order *stew*. The photograph shows the evidence. I even had a *cup of tea* AND bread and butter. They didn't have Daddy's sauce.

Flashback! Steve had somehow (he can't remember) gained ingression to a Roman widow's flat. She was sixty with a daughter and son. He had arranged for two of us to stay there the last three days of the leave. And so it came to pass. We left Eddie standing in his shirt – Angora, for the wearing of – standing by his bottom bunk saying, 'It's not fair, I'm not going to play with you any more.' Yes, we gave poor Eddie the elbow, and if he wasn't careful he'd get the shins and the knee bones as well.

Steve's suitcase has labels. Albergo Vittorio Emanuel, Albergo Grande Viale, Albergo Re de Italia, Albergo Savoia. It gives a touch of class to his 2/6 Marks and Spencer reinforced cardboard box with the knotted string handle.

It's in a faceless modern Mussolini-built block. We take the lift. 'What's this Primo Piano, Secondo Piano, Terzo Piano?' I told him that they had one piano on the first floor, two on the second and three on the third. Apartment 234. We are met at the door by the smiling grey-haired Roman widow. She's yours, I tell Steve. We are shown into the bedroom, and having dumped our kit, she gives us tea. Her husband had died just before the war in a car accident; she has a twelve-year-old son Raymondo and a twenty-one-year-old daughter Anna, who will be mine!

It was mid-afternoon and we went to the PICTURES! George O'Brien in *The Kid Rides West*. I had already seen him ride East, North and South, and the film was exactly the same except he did it in a different direction. It was full of 'Aw Shucks', 'You're looking real purty today Miss Lucy', and 'Are you a-callin' me a liar?' To the Alexander Club where my Hebrew friend did partake of Eggs and Chips. The REME band were playing. They were terrible. Someone shouted, 'Mend a lorry.' The band meant well, but then so did Hitler.

**Anna Morto**

Little did we know of the tragedy that was impending. On our return we were let into the flat by daughter Anna. 'Aye

Steve,' she said, and kissed him. 'This is my friend, Spike.'
Anna was tall, blue-eyed and blonde. She could have been a
model. Her brother is back from school, a dark lad with
numerous questions: 'Were we in the fighting, how was it,
had we won any battles?' It could have been any boy anywhere.

Anna works of an evening. Blast! Chance one gone! She
works in the American Officers' Club, the Nirvanetta. She is
bemoaning Rome's loss of elegance. She tells us that during
Mussolini's regime a woman was safe to walk anywhere after
dark, even during the German occupation, but now, she
threw her hands up in despair, now it was terrible, she
couldn't take the drunkenness and the lechery. Chance
number two gone. She wasn't joking, as we were to find out.

We were tired and after a shower I donned my terrible 'Made-out-of-cheap-sheet-then-dyed-with-a-dye-that-
comes-off-in-bed' pyjamas. I was reading old English newspapers and magazines from home. I must have dozed off and
I was awakened by Anna coming into my room. She put her
finger to her lips for silence, then whispered: 'Can I borrow
this chair?' Yes. Did she want to borrow me? I had two legs
less, but I was willing to be sat on. No. I was the last one to
see her alive.

At seven next morning, Raymondo burst into my room:
'Anna Morto,' he shouted. I leapt from my bed and followed
him to the kitchen. Anna was in the chair, a gas pipe leading
from the stove to her mouth. Hurriedly I picked her up. It
was horrible; rigor mortis had set in, and she stayed in the
shape of a person seated. Steve put the mirror to her mouth.

The mother is distraught, and that poor boy, that little
innocent face as yet unused to a world without a father, now
his sister . . . The mother says she has sent for the police. It
would be best if we weren't found here. We leave in embarrassing haste with our pyjamas under our battledress. I
often wonder if having two Allied soldiers in her home was
the last straw for Anna. Please God, I hope not. I will never
know. How insensitive we were. We never even went back or
wrote or said thank you. What kind of a person was I . . .?

It put a terrible damper on the rest of the holiday and soon we were in the lorry rumbling back to our Alma Mater, Maddaloni. Trouble with lorries is you can only see out of the back. 'You see where you've been and you already know that,' says the Yew.

Sometimes – on a dark night – I still see Anna's face.

## April 17

MY DIARY: MY BIRTHDAY. I'M 27. HAD EXTRA CUP OF TEA.

The news tells us that the Germans in Italy are on their last legs.

---

### Führer Bunker

HITLER IS IN THE KARZI GIVING HIMSELF ONE OF DOCTOR MORRELL'S ENEMAS.

ADOLPH: Allez oops! Ahhh! Dat is better.

GOEBBELS: Mein Führer, mein Führer.

ADOLPH: Dere's only one of me.

GOEBBELS: In Italy our troops are running out of legs.

ADOLPH: You Schwein, you haff ruined my happy enema hour.

---

*

I see Thelma Oxnevad. 'Spike, did you enjoy your leave?' Never mind that, Thelma, marry me at eight o'clock tonight. QMS Ward is asking me to come back to the band. I say, what about my impending coronary? He says that's all shit. As a qualified Quarter Master Sergeant he says I'm fit. But playing the trumpet could kill me! Yes it could, but if I take the risk, so will he. OK, I'll try. There I'll be, playing a great Bunny Berrigan chorus, I hit a top G, clutch my heart and crash face downwards on a mattress. ATS Candy Withers will raise my lovely head in her arms. Have I any last request? Yes, yes, yes, if she could just take her clothes off.

Also my thespian talents are in demand! Sergeant Lionel Hamilton thinks I could play a part in *The Thread of Scarlet*. Will I be the knot? We start rehearsing, but that old Black Magic called Manic Depression attacks me and I'm put to bed with *Aspirins*. What a doctor, I suppose he's still practising. God knows, he needs to. The play goes on, and horror of horrors, it's a success!

Someone is worse off than me. Mussolini has been murdered; he and his mistresses are hanging upside down in a garage in Milan.

*The Mussolini Massacre. They shoot horses, don't they?*

It was a barbaric act that puts the clock back. However, the natives seem happy. Nothing like an assassination to cheer the masses.

## May 1

MY DIARY: IT'S OVER! JERRY SURRENDERS!

I had just sat down at my morning desk still reeking of porridge when a very excited Colonel Startling Grope thundered into the office. 'Have you heard Terence? It's over! I've just spoken to Alex at AFHQ and it's OVER! General Vietinghoff von Nasty is at the Palace *now* signing the surrender.'

'Great! Do I have to sign anything, Stanley Sir? I mean, *I* haven't agreed to the surrender.' We can have the day off, he's right, it's time we had it off. The Ities are in the street singing 'Finito, Benito Finito' and 'Lae thar piss tub darn bab'. The bells of the churches ring out their iron victory message.

I walked back through the milling streets, lay on my bed and lit up a Capstan. I could hear the din outside and running footsteps, but I was strangely quiet. Suddenly a complete change of direction. How do you handle the end of a Campaign? I wanted to cry. Was it really over? 31,000 Allied troops had died – a city of the dead. Is a war ever really over?

A few days pass and Steve comes into the room. He is grinning: 'Have you seen? He's dead.' He shows me the headlines. '"HITLER. SUICIDE IN BUNKER." Yes, he's dead, his tart *and* his bloody dog.' He hammered the words out like nails in a coffin.

I had better news. Back at the officers' club in Portici I had snaffled a bottle of Dom Perignon 1935. 'I've been saving this, Steve,' I said, producing the bottle from its wrapper. We toasted the end in our enamel mugs. We sat grinning in silence. It was all too much; two soldiers; just statistics; where did we fit in . . .? Mind you, they were still fighting in Berlin, but most of the orchestra had stopped playing.

The Russians are sweeping into Berlin. Their might is awesome. The Allies and the Russians meet on the Elbe. At Lüneburg Heath, Monty accepts the German surrender. It's over. Just like that. One day war, the next it's peace. It's almost absurd. The entire energy of O2E is vested in preparations for the official V-E Night celebrations. It would appear that only alcohol can generate true happiness: hundreds of bottles, barrels and fiasco are stock-piled in every available area. They are scrubbing out the fountain! Why? It's the brainchild of RSM Warburton who has ordained that it be 'filled with wine'. They had tried to get the fountains to gush, but the plumbing had long since decayed. The date is fixed. In Part Two orders.

YOU *WILL* ALL HAVE A GOOD TIME,
YOU *WILL* GET DRUNK, AND YOU WILL
ALL STAGGER AROUND . . . YOU WILL
GET SICK OVER EACH OTHER FOR YOUR
KING AND COUNTRY. THE BAND WILL
PLAY FOR DANCING UNTIL 2 A.M.

*Space for being sick in .*

Chez Nous - 1944

Best Wishes from

Do you remember where your room was situated

The Square in Alexander Barracks

'Where did all those bloody Union Jacks come from?' Steve is counting the mass of flags that are now starting to appear around the barracks.

'Doesn't it make you feel good,' I said, 'to know that, despite it all, there are factories still making the British Flag.'

'Oh yes, there's nothing like a good old Union Jack to cheer you up.'

'I always carried a photo of the flag, and many a dark night in a muddy trench, I've taken it out and said to my trench mate: "Cheer up," and shown him my Union Jack. There would always be a response.' Wait! American flags are appearing. 'My God,' I cry out, 'they're running out of Union Jacks . . .!' It's getting bad! Italian flags are being hoisted, Russian! Any minute now the Ovaltinies' emblem will be shown. Janker wallahs on ladders are putting up hurriedly painted banners. VICTORY IN EUROPE! others: WELL DONE O2E! A large board with a hand giving the Victory salute. It's all happening.

I was still wondering if my brother had survived the last days of fighting. I saw him in Sydney last year and he was still alive. At the time I did not know he was still alive in Sydney.

## Tuesday 8 May

Official Victory celebrationsssssss, commence! It starts with the day off. We can obtain breakfast up to and including ten hundred hours.

Space for day off.

BILL of FARE

Assorted Sandwiches.

Jam Doughnuts

Mince Pies

Flapjacks

Custard Tart

Sausage Rolls

Vanilla Slice

Chelsea Buns

Fruit Flan

Tea    Coffee    Cocoa

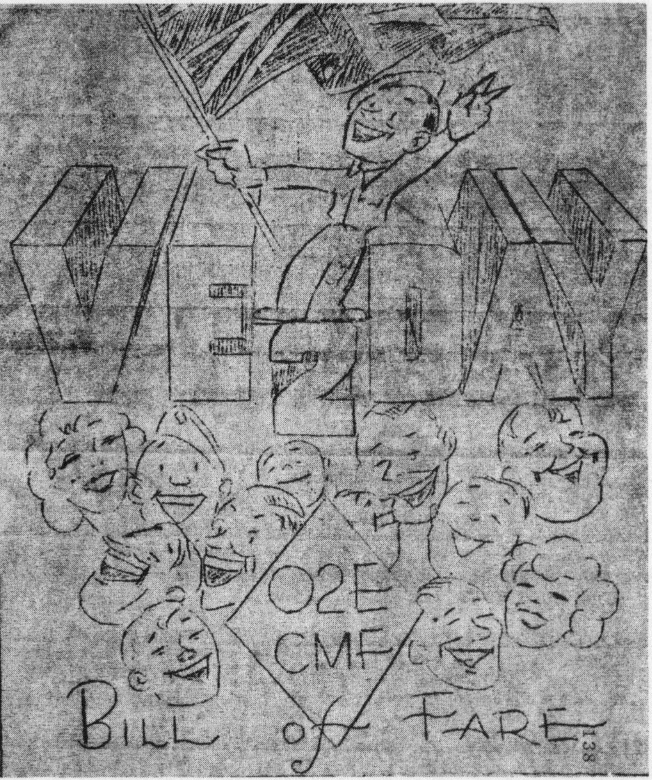

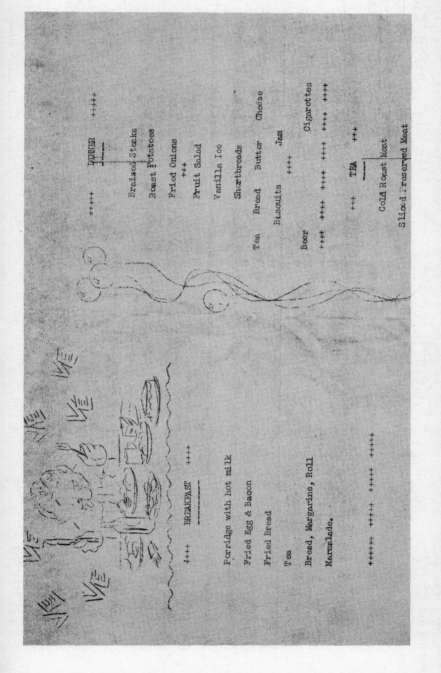

**BREAKFAST**
----------

++++ ++++

Porridge with hot milk

Fried Egg & Bacon

Fried Bread

Tea

Bread, Margarine, Roll

Marmalade.

+++++ ++++ +++++ +++++

**DINNER** ++++

+++++ +++++

Braised Steaks

Roast Potatoes

Fried Onions
+++

Fruit Salad

Vanilla Ice

Shortbreads

Tea   Bread   Butter   Cheese

Biscuits   Jam
+++

Beer   Cigarettes
++++ ++++ ++++ ++++ ++++

++   **TEA** +++

+++

Cold Roast Meat

Sliced Preserved Meat

Sergeant Beaton gives a long thanksgiving speech: 'Let us be grateful for this Victory.' We were grateful when he'd finished. On the hills behind the town, the Italians are climbing up to make a giant bonfire for the evening, a prelude to which is the occasional trial firework exploding in the street. We wash, rinse and sterilize our mess tins, then wipe them dry with disease-ridden teacloths. Years later, Peter Sellers told me that on this identical day, he was in Ceylon, telling an R A F M O that he (Sellers, that is) had heard a tiger outside his hut the previous night. There being no tigers in Ceylon, L A C Sellers was recommended for a Psychiatrist's Report. Alas, what transpired at that session has never been recorded.

PSYCHIATRIST:    Aircraftsman Sellers, you say that you've been hearing tigers.

SELLERS:    Yes, sir, there was one outside my hut.

PSYCHIATRIST:    Do you know there are no tigers in Ceylon?

SELLERS:    Well there are now.

PSYCHIATRIST:    It says, and I quote: 'I *heard* a tiger growling.'

SELLERS:    Yes sir.

PSYCHIATRIST:    You're sure it wasn't some other carnivore? I mean, lots of growls sound the same.

SELLERS:    Not this one, sir, this growl had stripes on.

At immediately-it-was-ready, the festivities started.

The Dance Hall is packed. For the first time Italian civilians are allowed in. A drunken fug hangs over everything. They've been drinking since dawn. In Alexander Square tables are laid with myriad edibles, a display that would have been a feast in rationed England. Fairy lanterns bedeck the trees, wine is flowing freely and the fountain is full of red chianti. It looks wonderful. On the hill the giant bonfire is alight. Fireworks are exploding in the streets under the great display of orchestrated electric lights.

*V-E Night in Merry Maddaloni*

We've never played so good. Charlie Ward sings: 'We're gonna get lit up when the lights go on in London.' It's like an anthem. A great chorus comes from the dancers. Colonel Startling Grope has sent us up six bottles of Asti Spumante! The evening wears on, the dancers wear out. A G I joins us. His name is Ken Mulé. He sings with the band. What a find – he sounds like Dick Haymes! More booze is coming up, but I'm keeping mine down. At two o'clock the dance finishes, but some of the band are 'into it' and go on jamming. I creep off and accost lovely Rosetta Page. We get a plate of sandwiches and a bottle of Valpolicella. Soon we are snogging.

'Oh, no, Spike, oh no.'

'Oh yes, Rosetta, oh yes.'

The sandwiches are crushed between us and are toasted.

'No ladies allowed in male billets.' The voice comes from the mouth under the little moustache of a Regimental Policeman.

'Haven't you heard? The war's over.'

'Never mind that, out!' He makes a gesture.

I am not a violent man. I take him by the battledress and crash him against the wall. 'Do you want to fuckin' die?' He doesn't want to die, and leaves.

Drink, drink, drink. Giggle, grope . . . Somewhere in the wee hours a long way away, sitting on the steps, someone is shaking me. It was me! No! It was Steve! He is naked except for his shirt. 'Rosetta darling,' I say, 'how you've changed.'

He giggles. 'Isn't it time you went to bed?' Yes. I was up about midday, surveying the wreckage of the previous night – most of which appeared to be me.


## 2nd Day of V-E Festivities

'A band from the Central Pool of Artists will play tonight, so you chaps can have a jolly good rest,' says Major New.

I'm lying in bed that morning 'resting', but for the love of me I don't feel good. I feel myself all over but none of me

*The CPA band that played on V-E Night + 1. The picture has been shrunk owing to financial difficulties at the publishers.*

feels good. I seek out Rosetta! Is she free tonight, or is she charging? Sorry, she's got a date at Caserta Palace. So! She's being unfaithful to me. Is it another man? No, it's another Regiment.

'Darling, will you be my first wife?'

Never mind, there's other distractions like housey-housey in the canteen, run by Sergeant 'Dolly' Grey, the Robert Maxwell of Maddaloni. 'And another little dip,' he cackled. 'Number nine, doctor's orders.' As the afternoon wore on and his winnings mounted, I saw him visibly changing into a bent, hand-rubbing, cackling Scrooge. By five o'clock it was 'Castor oil' – we'd been cleaned out. I walked out with ten lire which had the purchasing power of a bootlace. Lewis! The Yew! *He'd* have shekels. Yes, he'll lend me two thousand lire – after all, we were friends. I would just sign this paper consigning my entire worldly goods to him in the event of non repayment. So, as a bonded warehouse owned by Lewis, I went with him to the A F H Q Victory ball. Wow! Walking up those steps!

**Caserta** · Palazzo Reale · Scalone (prospetto)

The sound of a dance band wafts through the corridors. A girl is singing 'I was taken for a sleigh ride in July'. It sounds good. What a surprise! It's an all-American all-girl orchestra led by (it was a well-known name but I can't remember!) – some of you may remember, their signature tune was 'In the Blue of the Evening' or, if you're colour blind, the Brown of the Evening. They are all dressed in ice-white gowns looking like all-American women. Vestal virgins, hygienically wrapped, untouched by human hand, about to be debased in a TV series called Dysentery.

Such a cosmopolitan crowd! Greek sailors, Polish colonels, Yugoslavian partisans, Italian generals, Hindu captains, or as my father would say, a bunch of Wogs. Oh! the fun a xenophobe could have had with a shot gun! 'Who's paying for all this?' said Steve, as we raped the buffet table of food and wine.

I manage to get an American WAC. 'Do you like waltzes?'

I asked, avoiding 'Harry Lauder appeared in Glasgow' routine. 'Nhart Rilly,' she said. (Not Really, she said.)

'Where are you from?'

'The Yewknighted Staits.'

I guessed that, I said. Then why did I ask? She works as a 'Clurk to Generil Muark Clurk'. I estimated her typing speeds would be anything up to several words a day. A Pakistani orderly cuts in. Just wait till she sees his, I thought.

'We're supposed to be having a good time,' said Steve, guzzling Asti Spumante.

'Yes, I suppose this is a good time,' I said, guzzling Asti Spumante.

'Are you suggesting it could be better,' he said, guzzling Asti Spumante.

'Well it would be nice if we could find a couple of birds,' I said, guzzling Asti Spumante. 'What I need is Romanceeeee.' And what do I get? – a Yewish Sergeant and Asti Spumante!

We bustle our way out to the rear gardens. There is a sea of tables with candles. We choose one and Asti Spumante. It's a warm May night, the sound of the fountains is interwoven with the dance music. Lewis dumps a large jug of wine on the table. 'Reinforcements,' he says. I have run out of money again. Would Steve give me a mortgage on my parents? We take a stroll on the great lawns. 'It's all mad, isn't it?' says Steve. 'I mean we don't belong here. This,' he makes a sweeping gesture, 'this is where the Bourbons and their satin ladies should be cavorting.'

He was right. 'We are out of time with this place,' I said. 'We belong at the WVS with Egg and Chips.'

There we are, wiping the eggs from the plate with bread in the canteen with the Italian Manageress with the huge bum. It ought to be in *The Guinness Book of Records*, but right now it's in Caserta. 'Two teas, signorina,' says Steve. I light up a cigarette, sip tea. We both sit staring, that end-of-the-day stare. You see it in pubs, tubes, restaurants, intervals at the theatre; always looking away from the company you're in; something out there that will make the present more exciting? Curiosity killed the cat? It may have found a better

See page 120 for details

cat. My watch says V-E night plus one is over, and we are in tomorrow. My God, it's all going to happen again. I rise from my seat, clutch the air and moan. 'The filessss, the filessss.'

'Yes,' said Steve, 'it's time for beddy-byes so you'll be a nice strong boy for your filing.'

I put on my beret, that bloody awful new beret! They had taken our forage caps from us and given us a thing that looked like a pudden cloth, or something that Auntie Rita wore to visit the Geriatric Ward. No matter how you wore it, it looked like a cow pat stuck on your head, about to slide off down your face.

The passion wagon drops us at Alexander Barracks. The

roistering is in full flood and sounds like a farmyard on fire. One last drink, my friend.

'Ahhh Terence!' It's Colonel Startling Grope. 'Where have you been hiding these last two days?'

I tell him. 'In my beret, Stanley Sir.' Come on, have a Strega with him.

'Cheers Terence!' He holds up the yellow liquid. 'It's all over.' He was right, most of it went over him.

The night died like a beheaded chicken; long after the head was off, the body went on dancing. I lay in bed, the distant sound of the CPA dance band echoing up the stairs . . .

## Peace

To the victor the spoils. My spoils are a set of files. Big News! Startling Grope is leaving us.

'I'm being bowler-hatted,' he said. (*I* thought he would have been brown-hatted.) 'I leave next week, Terence, and,' he tapped his nose, it stayed on, 'I've left you a little present.'

Me? A present? What is it, a pot of Gentlemen's Relish? A Unique Device with latent Screws? A Germolene dispenser? A leather-backed Divining Kit, a complete set of Marshmallows, a Devious Appliance with lubricating points? Any of these could be mine!

'Who's taking your place here, Stanley Sir?'

'Nobody.'

'Well that doesn't speak very well of you.'

'The job is being run down, Terence.'

'It was more than run down, it's down right crummy.'

So departed the Colonel, and the pretty boys of 02E breathed a sigh of relief. Bending down would never be as dangerous again.

# The Great Neapolitan Band Contest

56 Area are holding a Dance Band Contest. We'll wipe the floor with 'em. FIRST PRIZE FOR SUPERB LEAD AND SOLO TRUMPET, GUNNER MILLIGAN. We congregate in the rehearsal room. What to play?

'What's wrong with Dinah?' says Manning.

'Rheumatism,' is the answer. We choose 'Moonlight Serenade', 'Two O'clock Jump' and 'The Naughty Waltz'.

'You see! Those numbers will lose us the contest,' predicts Jim, one of the first people in 1939 to say 'The war will be over by Christmas.' We practise and practise, every note and nuance is observed, we even play the specks of fly shit that land on the music. Nothing is wasted.

We want to wear just shirts and trousers. Major New won't hear of it: 'This is a military occasion, and you will look regimental.' OK, we can wear steel helmets, full pack, and play in the kneeling loading position; then while half of the band play 'Moonlight Serenade', the other half dig slit trenches; in 'One O'clock Jump' we can all fix bayonets and charge the judges; and finally, in 'The Naughty Waltz' we'll all crawl along the stage and lob grenades at the audience.

The time is come. Backstage, musicians with extra Brylcreem in their dressing-rooms, playing scales, octaves or cards. Major New announces the draw. 'We're on first.' Groans.

'I told you we'll 'ave no luck with those fuckin' numbers,' says Manning.

'It's Kismet,' I said.

'What?'

'Kismet, that's what Nelson said to Hardy.'

'I thought it was Kiss Me Hardy.'

No, that was Stan Laurel, that's the popular version, you're very popular if you quote that version.

'U lot better get on,' says a snotty-nosed Base Depot Sergeant, one of those cringing acolytes that has always got extra fags and chocolates in their locker, a housey-housey

# Dance band contest gets away on the down beat

*1945*

AN innovation in Naples entertainment was the 56 Area Welfare Services' Dance Band Competition, at the Bellini Theatre on Sunday. It was a big success, both as an interesting competition and as a well-staged show.

The compere was Capt. Philip Ridgway, son of Philip Ridgway of the famous radio show.

Each of the eight bands had a strong following.

The bands were called upon to play a slow fox-trot, a modern waltz and a quick-step as competitive pieces. This gave scope for sweet music as well as swing, and generally the standard of playing was very high.

Marks were awarded for intonation, tempo, phrasing and attack, and ensemble—and though these finer points were perhaps above a large part of the audience, there seemed common concurrence with the judges' decisions.

The first band on the stage was G.H.Q. O2E, led by Sjt. Stan Britton, and it achieved the difficult task of building up the right atmosphere and setting the feet of the audience tapping. There followed:—

"F" Section, 16 Base Workshops (leader Cfn. Jack Sheldon); The Pionians, 338 (A) Company, Pioneer Corps (Hans Tischard); 5 Assembly Wing, Type A I.R.T.D. (Sjt. Reg Service); 8 Petrol Depot, R.A.S.C. (Pte. Jack Curtiss); 5 Bn., No. 1 G.R.T.D. (Pte. Eddie Williams); 113 M.U., R.A.F. (L.A.C. Lee Underwood); and "J" Section, 750 Base Workshops R.E.M.E. (Cfn. Mack Loveday)

Lieut. T. T. Short, 56 Area's producer, saw to it that there was no delay in changing bands, and the whole show went "to tempo."

The judges, carefully chosen for the job, were Lieut. Eddie Carrol, the B.B.C. dance band leader, Lieut. "Spike" McIntosh, well-known locally as a trumpeter and Ensa's C.M.F. Publicity Officer, and F.-O. Laurie Blewis, producer of M.C.A.F. entertainments.

Three bands—5 Assembly Wing, I.R.T.D.; 113 M.U., R.A.F.; and 16 Base Workshops pass into the semi-final to be held on Sunday, June 10, for dancing in the ballroom at the Royal Palace Naab. It will begin at 1900 hrs.

The judges added that O2E were close runners-up. As opening band they had perhaps been handicapped but the order of playing had been decided by draw.

Individual awards were:— 113, M.U., R.A.F. Cpl. Dennis Jones (tenor sax); and Cpl. Eric Chapman (trumpet). 5 Assembly Wing, L.-Cpl. H. Burn section leader (trumpet). 5 Bn. G.R.T.D., Pte. Eddie Williams (piano), and Pte. Sid Grainger (drums). 8 Petrol Depot, Dvr. Dennis Ewart (alto sax). Pionians, L.-Cpl. Kurt Braun (vocalist). O2E, Sjt. Harry Carr, section leader (alto sax).

Prizes for instrumentalists will be presented at the final, at the Bellini Theatre, on Sunday, June 17.

NORMAN ENGLAND.

137

concession, never lends money, and has never been nearer than a hundred miles to the front line.

The compère for the contest is Captain Philip Ridgeway, the announcer. He is as informed on Dance Bands as Mrs Thatcher is on Groin Clenching in the Outer Hebrides. Other judges are Lt. Eddie Carrol, famed composer of 'Harlem' and Lieutenant 'Spike' Mackintosh, famous for not writing 'Harlem'.

Can you believe it – we didn't win! WE DIDN'T WIN!!! I wasn't even *mentioned*!! Why were the 56 Area Welfare Service persecuting me like this? At the contest I had heard shouts of 'Give him the Prize'. No one listened, even though I shouted it very loud. Never mind, there would be other wars . . .!

The first Dance Band Contest held in this country took place at the Bellini Theatre on Sunday, 3rd June. Eight bands took part, including the O2E Dance Band, and a very high standard was shown by most of the competitors.

Each band played four numbers, the first being a "warm-up" followed by a Slow Foxtrot, Waltz and Quickstep.

The O2E Band opened the contest, their combination being 3 Trumpets, 2 Alto Sax, Tenor Sax, Piano, Drums, Bass and Guitar, and for their three tunes they chose "Moonlight Serenade," "Naughty Waltz," and "Two O'Clock Jump."

They had a great reception, which they richly deserved. Every man gave of his best and the intonation and phrasing were excellent. "Two O'Clock Jump" was the most difficult piece played during the contest, and was tackled with exceptional aptitude.

*Excerpt from* Valjean *by S. G. Lewis*

I took it all philosophically. I dressed up as Plato. So what? I didn't get a prize, but I still had my files, my pile ointment and my treasure trove of back-up underwear; mine would get anybody's back up.

Now I would concentrate on chasing Candy; evidence of this is contained in the following drool document:

138

Sunday, 45.

I'd met her — at once it was plain
to me — I was very much in love —
or love with fear — but I simply
had to call her Candy. I'd wrote her
a little meditation — (not the work
of genius you afraid) I asked her to read
it on Sunday during her visit — I made
her promise to destroy it — I thought she
might laugh at it — show it to her
friends — but — she did not laugh
she did not show it to scoffing eyes —
I pleaded not destroy it — she said
it had meant something to her — I was
deliriously happy — the following day
I received a note asking the meaning
of it all — I was so taken off
of my balance — I never dreamed
I could arouse her interest (or any girl's
for that) — so I wrote a magic new
poem and included a request for a
date — I saw Candy again next day
she had read my note — the answer
came — a nod of her head — ZING!!
I was a god — a genius — I was —
I was walking on frosted pastures of silver —
oh heavens! how my heart soared —
I tried to act casual when I said
to her — I'll see you to-night at 7? — "Yes"
Yes!! — how easy it could have been
for her to say no!! but no it was Yes!
Oh Candy — you have pierced me round
and spun — night & day — and we
went breezy up some road — I don't know

where — all I wanted to hear was her
voice — seeing her I feel her once are one —
we caught a small wood —
their led into a — field with
cornfields — we sat on a bank —
I weary years in uniform and
this was my happiest night —
we talked thus endlessly talked —
a new envoy — civil jumps — and
all the time Candy was there — at
last I pulled her longer over it —
I kissed her cheek — soft a
Petal of geranium — Grace
I wanted to tell her — Candy I
love you — but — well I just could not —
we laughed & kissed — and I kissed her
on her red mouth — the top of
Vesuvius was a cold place at that moment —

Did you get that? Did I really write that crap? No wonder the BBC only book me on a pro-rata basis. That Milligan of 1945 is dead. Then I was twenty-seven. Now I am sixty-seven and the engine has just had its tenth MOT test and failed.

## June 17

DIARY: DANCE BAND FINALS

We sat through the finals contest, disenchanted that we weren't in it, but drew comfort when Taffy Carr was called: '1st Prize for the best lead alto, Sergeant H. Evans 02E band,' and was handed something that had been made by St Dunstan's Home for the Blind. It looked like an army tea mug with the handle removed, stuck on to a sawn-down broom handle nailed to the lid of a cigarette tin, then white-washed. 'It'll look good on the mantelpiece,' said Taffy. I for one couldn't wait. He threw a celebration dinner, most of which hit Jim Manning. No, seriously folks, at La Topo off Via Roma we spaghettied and wined too much, but at the time it seemed just right. All stuffed into a brougham, pulled by a thin horse, we sang and shouted, until, on a hill, the horse packed in. We paid the driver. When he saw the tip – he packed it in as well. Three in the morning, I tiptoed in.

'Who's that?' said the Yew clutching his Pay Book.

'Steve, you've been waiting for me like a good Jewish mother.'

'I hope it was a *nice Jewish girl*,' was all he would say.

Now, *I* would raise the band's morale! For one, they looked terrible playing in battledress. And they looked terrible when they were not playing.

I chat up a local tailor. Can he make Harry James white jackets like my drawing? 'Si.' Armed with the 'Si', I troop all the herberts back to be measured.

'Is 'e a tailor or a mortician?' says Jim.

'You must wait and see, Jim.'

'Who's going to bloody well pay?' says sensible Stan Britton.

'We must wait and see,' I tell him.

The jackets are splendid; it only remains for us to dye our trousers black, draw white shirts from the Q Stores, buy bow ties, and no one will be able to tell the difference between Harry James and us, provided they stand well back. It's a secret.

When the curtains part at the Saturday hop, gasps of 'We're in the wrong hall' come from the dancers. ''Tis a miracle,' says an Irishman, crossing himself.

Major New comes puffing up. 'Bai Jove laids, you look super, this is how I always wanted the boys to look.'

Thank you, we say, and that will be ten thousand lire a jacket; and lo! the Major is cast down – but in the goodness of time he payeth up, and lo, there was a great skint in the

The O2E Dance Band

Piano S. Britton.    C. Ward.    J. Manning.    Harry Evans    S. Milligan
Drums. V. Shewen.    Guitar. Bill    Bass. L. Prosser.

141

camp. However, *he* got all the bloody praise, *and* took it. At dinner, the Brigadier made a speech: here it is, as reported by an officers' mess waiter, Private Rossi.

Gentlemen, I'd just like to thank Major New for his brilliant transformation of the band from sacks of shit to Harry James sacks of shit. The design of white jacket and black trousers showing where the top half leaves off and the bottom half begins is a great help to musicians when dressing themselves.

Every word is true, I swear on this copy of *Portnoy's Complaint*.

Looking as good as we did, the gigs rolled in, and for a gunner I was getting rich. The going rate was now 500 lire or the equivalent in force feeding. There were better things to come.

## LIAP

Yes, L I A P – laugh you fools! To you L I A P means nothing but to us herberts in Italy it means Leave in Blighty! The home of Spotted Dicks and Treacle, Saveloy and Mushy Peas.

The withdrawal of the musicians from active service must be carefully planned, plinned and plonned! QMS Drew Taylor, our Svengali, has arranged a roster so that twixt July and October, the band will range from Full Orchestra in July, down to a selection from Piano, Drums, Bass and three Saxes, then just Piano and Double Bass in September. In October there would be one week with just a man banging a dustbin lid and whistling. It was better than nothing, but only just. The band felt a new importance. Without us, eighty per cent of entertainment was curtailed.

Why I was so overjoyed at the prospect of leave in the UK was silly. In Italy I was eating better, getting paid better and all in sunshine. No! it was that thing called 'home': wanting to get back to what it was before it all happened. Alas, there was no going back, ever. It would never be the same again for any of us. We were dreaming, chum. Now I furtively release this letter I wrote to my pal in 19 Battery, then 'somewhere in Holland':

MY DEAR OLD SPLATTER GUTZ,

ITS ABOUT TIME WE GOT IN CONTACT WITH EACH OTHER.
IT WAS NOT UNTIL THE OTHER DAY I WAS SURE WHERE THE REGIMENT WERE...YOU LOW
SKUM...STAND BACK HUP THERE....LEAVVE ME IN THIS STINKING HOLE WITH NO LETTERS?
HUP THERE...HI....HUP. SO YOU HAVE HAD LEAVE IN BLIGHTY...YOU LOW SOD HUP THERE
LILLHO....HUP THERE...STAND BACK WHILE HE ARISES....AND I SUPPOSE THERE WAS MUCH
NECKING WITH THE HACKER...EH??HUP THERE...HO...HI  YOU SKUMFILTH....AND DID Y
YOU ATTEMPT TO GET IN TOUCH WITH ME...DID YOU...F.....ARSOLES...HI..HUP THERE
...STAND BACK LET HIM UP...W.H.A.C.K.....TAKE THAT..WALLLOOOOPPPPP...SMAK....
YOU DONT LIKE IT.....KLUNK...( RIGHT ON HIS FILTHY CRUST) AND WHAT IS IT LIKE IN
BLA......???DONT TELL ME YOU SWINE...FILTHY BLACK DROOLING SWINE....BLAM...
RIGHT IN THE OLD BREAD BASKET...HI THERE HUP...HO...HOW IS THE OLD BAND GOING..
EH....OH ITS FINE ..WELL TAKE THAT...KLUD SPLAT.RIGHT IN THE KNACKERS...
HO HO HIS FACE IS TURNING A TRIFLE BLUE.....AND IT CANT BE THE COLD SIR....
YOUR PHOTO WAS IN THE "TATLER WITH THE REST OF THE CONCERT PARTY A LA ROMA...
YOUVE SEEN IT EH????WELL TAKE THAT...BLATSMAZSH....RIGHT BETWEEN THE EYS....
HO THERE HUP ITS YER OLD FORGOTTEN DUSKY PAL SPIKE....CLANG...UNDER THE SHIN
WITH A BRASS ROLLING PIN....HA IT HURTS....WHACK.WHACK. WHACK...HEH HEH HEH...
TEE HEE HEE......MY BROTHER DESMOND IS IN HAMBURG..IN THE OX AND BUCKS...TRY AND
LOOK HIM UP.....TAKIING OF LOOKING UP ..LOOK AT THAT AEROPLANE......KRUNCH SPLAT
RIGHT IN THE GLOTTIS...HO THERE HUP ...HI AND AWAY TO THE SPANISH TWIST PIPE.
I'M BACK IN CIRCULATION ON THE HORN...AND LEADING A 4 PIECE BRASS SECTION...
PLUS FOUR SAXES....WE CAME 4th IN THE ALD ITALY CONTESY...OH YOU HAVENT HEARD ABO
UT IT WELL.....ZONOKLUD.....FOR YOU STUPID OLD ARSE.......AND IM IN AGE GROUP
28......SO ILL BE GOING HOME ABOUT THE SAME TIME AS YOU...WE WILL HAVE A PARTY
WITH A BIG CLUB IN THE CORNER....AND DO YOU KNOW WHT HAPPENS WHEN THE LIGHTS GO
OUT...????YOU MAKE A GRAB FOR HACKER...BUT DO YOU REACHER.?.HO HO NO NO HI HUP
THERE....DONG...RIGHT ON YOUR CRUST COMES THE LAVISH KNOWLEDGED NAIL FILLED CLUB
....OH OOOOOOOOOOOHHHH MY POOR BATTERED CRUST YOU MOAN....HEE HEE WHACK...
AND ALL IS QUITE BAR THE MONOTOUS KLUNK OF THE KLUB ON YOUR KRUST!!!. EVERY ONE IS

Calligraphy experts have described the handwriting as 'critical', and who are we to argue with qualified nursing sisters?

While waiting for L I A P, we continue to play for dances, but as the photo shows I have been promoted to the right, so I am within hitting distance of the pianist.

*The new white jacket band on a cloth of gold, plus a moustache . . .*

Notice too I have grown a moustache, brass players swear it: 'bound the embouchure'. It made me swear, a *real* bloody bind, and shaving became difficult, but, you see, Robert Taylor had grown one and I couldn't let him get away with it.

## The Torch of Love is Extinguished

One letter did it. Lily Dinley is getting married! That's bad enough, but, to another *man*. That's terrible. This was the girl I had carried a torch for. Though she had officially left me, I lived in hopes that one day she'd officially come back, if only to get the money I owed her. I prayed she would change her mind or her body; as long as the latter stayed the same shape as when I last saw it at 47 Revlon Road, Brockley – it was better than egg and chips. Anyway, her letter sent me into the depths of depression and when I arrived, no one was down there. This letter lets in the light for you dear dear

145

BDR TA MILLIGAN      5 1945

954024

O BRANCH . GHQ  2nd Echelon

CMF .

1945

Dear Old Boy,

A thousand pardons for failing to write to you for so long....
when I explain the reason you will understand only too well.....Lily got
married about two months back , and I have been on the booze ever since...
honest son, nothing ever hit me so hard....I worshipped that girl in my own
peculiar fashion...lets forget it eh?.  I supose you have heard about the

well old Harry, I'm going home to Blighty in three weeks time....What are the
chances of seeing you old son??? I will drop in and see you people in any case .
Its raining oceans in Italy to day. Harry I will be hoping to settle down in
N London after the war..(On my own) so i would like very much to be seeing a
lot of you and your gang at my place (where ever that is)..I dont quite know
what I'm going to do without Lily.......9 Years is a long time to be in love
with one girl......Lets forget it.......I want you to give all the following RTO

NASH, and any that I may have forgotten. WELL XXXXX Harry I am in the dumps
..I dont know what the hell I'm going to do on leave...I have no bloody home
to go to and the girl ?..ha ha what a bloody mockery life is .....dont take
any notice of the depression I6m laying on, write soon harry...

Your Sincere friend

Spike

readers. I've excised certain parts which would not interest you; they just contained certain private measurements.

Students of punctuation will be rolling on the floor.

But despite Lily, I was still writing to my harem in the UK – Beryl, Bette, Mae, Ivy; there were shortages in England, but not of this.

Zounds! It's too much to believe. 'The Band are to have a week's leave in Rome,' says Major New. 'It's for the good work you've all done.'

I didn't understand. We'd never done any work. As if this is not enough, dear reader, on the 23 July my life is enriched by the legacy of Startling Grope. He's left orders that from this day henceforth I am to be promoted to Unpaid Acting Bombardier. No money, but I can put two stripes on my sleeve and I don't have to curtsy to Sergeants any more. Startling Grope has his little joke, for one day later . . . I am now PAID BOMBARDIER!

'Someone has blundered,' says Sergeant Britton, who is now only one stripe ahead! I catch lovely long Captain Thelma Oxnevad. I show her my two stripes. 'Any chance now?' I say, but before she can answer me I am laid low – not by illness, no, by treatment. Typhus inoculation. First shot.

'Roll your sleeve up,' said a Medical Orderly. 'Just a little prick.'

I said I could see he was.

'Can you feel that?' he said.

'Yes, coming out the other side.'

He was well pleased.

Soon I'm in bed with a high temperature.

'Have you heard the news?' says Steve, holding up a paper.

I listen. I can't hear anything. What's he mean? I *am* the news.

'They've dropped the Atom Bomb.'

Very good Steve, but *who's* dropped it on *who*? The Yanks! Of course! They've got the money. He held up the paper.

'ATOM BOMB DROPPED IN HIROSHIMA'. I was delirious and really didn't give a bugger.

'It's their own bloody fault,' I said.

## August 9

DIARY: BOOSTER INOCULATION

Ouchhhhhh! He was still a little prick. This time it was worse, a hundred and three temperature!

'At least you keep the room warm at night,' says Lewis.

Sadist! The Rev. Sergeant Beaton hears my groans and comes to minister the last rites. He's disappointed, I'll live. 'Whisky in hot tea is good for yew.'

I buy a bottle – it's good for me! And by the amount *he* drank, good for him. I have two doubles, then send out for hot tea. It's a knockout. While I sleep, another plane is on its way to Nagasaki. By the time I wake the city is no more and the nature of war is to become a nightmare, something that I was just coming out of. I'm pouring with sweat. I feel like a wet rag but can't find one anywhere. Nagasaki! That used to be the name of one of my favourite busking tunes!

> Hot ginger and Dynamite
> That's all they get at night
> Back in Nagasaki
> Where the fellas chew t'baccy
> And the women wiggy waggy woo.

I haven't heard that song since. Amazing how one atom bomb can kill a song writer's income.

I'm groggy in bed for a while. Steve is bringing my meals in, and eating them. 'How do you feel?'

'Hungry.'

'That doesn't leave much after tax,' he said, and I still don't understand what he meant.

'Stop that bloody noise in there,' shouts the Rev. Sergeant Beaton. 'We're trying to meditate.'

'Sorry,' says Steve. 'Let us know when it's our turn.'

## Roma Encore

The holiday with Scotland's Revenge (porridge) and Links of Love (Slingers). All packed and puffing cigarettes, our lorry drives out of Alexander barracks in triumph. As we pass through the proles on their way to their offices, they boo us. 'You wouldn't 'af to work if you'd learn the fiddle,' chortles Jim Manning. It's a glorious day with a sky like Canaletto; unlike England where it's like Cannelloni.

## September 1

DIARY: 56 AREA REST CAMP. LOVELY LAZY DAY. SWIMMING, GRUB, PICTURES, PING-PONG.

The consensus is we go to a restaurant. We find one in the Via Forno, a lovely little trattoria with plastic grapes hanging from the ceiling, raffia-bound flasks hanging in clusters from the wall, and candles on the table. Several blue-chinned mafia-style waiters are waiting to serve, or murder us. It's pasta all round, except for Jim Manning. He's not going to ''ave any of those long strips of garlic worms, no, it's egg and chips'. Alright, we can laugh – eggs are good for you, they give you the 'orn. I find a delightful red wine, Tignanello. Then two shillings a gallon, now £6 a bottle, I'm glad I ordered it then. We now rush rapidly to the next morning to avoid all that retching out of the back of the lorry.

## Diary: September 2

Terrible hangover. Felt better after breakfast. Lovely sunny day. It is now ALL over: the Nips have jacked it in.

'The bastards,' said Jim Manning. 'The bomb was too bloody good for 'em – they should have dropped something cheaper, like gas stoves filled with shit.' What a thought.

The Romans ignore the Victory, the Allied soldiers get pissed, the City is full of stumbling, staggering, farting drunks, none of whom have ever seen a Jap. The rest camp

*Funny ha-ha reaction to the End of W W II by Bdr. Milligan – note modern frizz-top hair-do. Left: Vic Shewery; right: Jim Manning who volunteered to pose with me.*

leaves the latecomers a huge table of the latest greatest horror in British cuisine, the dreaded Cold Collation, each plate containing the following:

> Small part of cold dead chicken.
> One lettuce leaf brown at edges.
> One slice of tomato laid like wreath
>   on dead chicken bit.
> Mess of diced stale boiled potatoes
>   hiding under thin watery mayonnaise.
> Sprig of watercress.
> Thin slice of bread curling at edges as
>   though about to fly off plate.
> Six pale peas glued together for security.
> A shrimp.
> Greasy thumbprint.

# NIPPON DAILY NEWS

**Emperor Hirohito hit by gas stove filled with shit. Western barbarians drop ultimate weapon. Despicable act without warning. No surrender. Antikarzi squadrons to intercept new hell weapon.**

It was a warm night and we all knew who had had brown ale. 'I think,' says Len Prosser, 'if they'd dropped Cold Collation on Hiroshima it would have done more damage.' He's right! After eating it, we surrendered.

There's no lights out, so we play Pontoon. At one in the morning, from distant campanili, a series of one o'clocks ring out over the rooftops of Rome. One o'clock went on for a good seven minutes. We set our watches some twenty times.

'It must be different religions,' I said, 'like the Protestants are three minutes behind the Greek Orthodox, and the Catholics one minute up on the Coptics.' They all say I'm a silly bugger.

'That's it,' says a triumphant Jim Manning. 'Pontoons only.' He scoops up the winnings.

I hadn't done too badly, I'd come out with the same amount I'd had before the game, but then I hadn't played – I'd had my fingers burnt before when someone set fire to the cards.

The days that followed were much the same. Monday, Tuesday etc. to the power of seven. Breakfast, lazing, swim, lunch, lazing, swim, cold collation, screaming, ping-pong, evening spruce up, Rome, sightseeing, pictures, dance, Trattoria, Alexander Club, pictures, cold collation, screaming, late night boozing, smoking, wanking, screaming.

# Diary: September 6

Last day! MUST do something. Breakfast, lazing, swim, lunch, lazing, breakfast, cold collation, screaming, wanking, lunch – elephant strangling in rum (eh?). I'd found a great 'Cinema Vérité' film, *Città Aperta*. No one wants to see it. 'It's in bleedin' Iti, isn't it?' says The Jim Manning. Yes, dear lad, would he like Cockney sub-titles? No – he's going to have egg, chips and the horn. It's a marvellous film, very, very moving, a wonderful performance by Aldo Fabrizi, and I came out depressed but elated.

I hie me to the Alexander Club, and there pleasure myself with choice teas and buns. A 'Naafi' pianist is playing, an assassination job; he does for music what Dracula did for anaemia. I stand and listen to the horror and realize what a good thing assassination is. To recover I have a carafe of wine and head for home.

Outside the streets are bright, shops are open late, streets bustle with night life. I'm looking in a ladies' lingerie shop with my memories. A voice behind me. 'Are you looking for a dirty girl?' It's a very beautiful thirty-year-old female.

No, I wasn't looking for a dirty girl, I was looking for some clean underwear. She smiled a ravishing smile and showed teeth as white as piano keys. She looked at me with huge brown eyes, a stunner. I had never been accosted before, I didn't know what to say; this was real men's stuff. My mother said I never should play with the gypsies in the wood. To hell with that.

Her name is Maria Marini (all gypsies not in the wood in Italy are called Maria). A high degree of naughty was possible! I asked her why she had chosen me. I looked kind. Kind? What kind? Her words: 'You looka nice.' The bottom drops out of the naughty when she tells me she's *not* a tart, *this* is the first time! Why, dear girl, are you doing this dreadful thing? Doesn't she know I'm trying to cure myself of Cold Collation, screaming and wanking? She's a teacher from the University of Milan, she was holidaying in Rome when the Germans put a curfew on all civilian movements. She was broke and desperate. I said so was I, I'd just had egg and chips. A friend had suggested there were two ways to make money, tarting or counterfeiting. Both ways you get fucked. When we got to her small but tidy flat overlooking the Basilica di Santa Maria Maggiore (all Basilicas not called Franco are called Maria in Italy), she broke down. Should I call the AA? I couldn't bring myself to do it folks. I slept on that sofa!

After a good night's Cold Collation and somnambulism, she brings me coffee and a slice of cake. I would have done better at the Rest Camp! 'Ta for not shagging me, now can I have the money,' she says, in so many words. She has thought twice about it, she wants me to stay! Has she caught a glimpse of it in the night? 'I ken be lak a waf to you,' she says. 'I ken cock for you.' Well, I'd love her to cock for me, but I have to leave – the people in Maddaloni are dancing to a man banging a dustbin lid as he whistles. Will I write to her? Yes, and send soap, chocolate and a few million lire. She will wait for me. As I leave she grabs me, kisses me, then slams the door on my fingers. I return to the camp with a bandaged hand and am greeted with, 'Did she 'ave barbed wire round it?' Tell them all, every sordid little detail.

I upgraded the story. She was a distressed Countess, she wanted me to live with her. Corrrrrrr! I could be the distressed Count. You count. She made me dress as Mussolini and make love to her! Corrr! I wrote to Maria for nearly two years and I met her again in Volume VI (Order your copy now – due 1986).


## September 6

It's back to Maddaloni and straight into the Junior Ranks Dance. The ATS are allowed to wear dresses, frocks, and what look like broken army blankets stitched together with boot laces. At the door they are all given a flower. The lighting would have done credit to any swish night club, and so much food and drink seemed evil. We play some new arrangements; including 'Star Eyes' which was great; here I am seen at my pristine best playing the muted Trumpet solo.

*Playing 'Star Eyes'. My eyes are closed to avoid seeing any Cold Collation.*

The dance contest is to be 'judged' by Brigadier Henry Woods CBE, which is no worse than Mary Whitehouse choosing the best porno movie. Groans follow his every decision but he goes merrily on giving marks for the dancer with the 'best haircut' in the Waltz, and 'best-polished shoes' in the Quick Step. It's the biggest débâcle since Dunkirk. By some miracle Rosetta Page wins the spot prize – she's covered in them. In my white Harry James jacket, dyed black trousers, bandaged hand and moustache, I manage to get the last waltz.

'What happened to your hand, Spike?'

I caught it on some barbed wire, I tell her. 'I'm going on leave. Will you miss me?' Of course she will, she makes a point of it.

A letter from a girlfriend, Beryl Southby, sends me news of a song contest being held at the Hammersmith Palais by Oscar Rabin. Immediately I am George Gershwin, Cole Porter and Irving Berlin. I see myself at a lonely piano on a grouse moor in pouring rain. Lit by a hurricane lamp, I am dressed as a damp Chopin. All through the tempest I cough blood, sip lemon tea and write a masterpiece of a tune called 'Dream Girl'. I write to my friend Gunner Edgington in distant Holland telling of my composition, a tune that is a sinecure for the depressed; one chorus will cure love sickness, two will stop varicose veins, three will prevent scrofula and psoriasis. The first prize is a thousand pounds. A thousand pounds; think what I could do with that! For a start, I could spend it. I send the song off. 'Dear Oscar, herewith the winner, signed Bombardier Milligan S.'

That was in 1945 . . . perhaps the post is slow. The winning song was 'Twitty Twitty Twink Twink means I love you'. Now you know what's wrong with the bloody country. At the time I *didn't* know what was wrong with the country, other than there was a great shortage. I for one wasn't getting enough of it.

## Little Bits of Useless Information

I had started to write essays (Essay, essay, essay, Who was that lady I saw you with last night . . .); these essays weren't like Lamb's, they were like Mutton. One was on the death mask of a young girl found drowned in the Seine in 1899. I was haunted by the smile on the dead girl's face. Where else did I expect to see it? In an Essay Contest run by Corporal Hewitt, I won nothing. I've kept it secret until now, under the Thirty-Year Release of Information for the Security of the Nation Act.

## A Trifle

Every morning a pretty Italian girl passed our office window. I would say 'Buon Giorno' to her through the bars of my window, and she would throw bread to me. I did this drawing of her, now released under the Release of Information for the Security of the Nation Act.

One morning as I called to her, she burst into tears. What

155

Senorina
Maddalena . Italy
1945

was wrong? Len Arrowsmith, married man, father and lecher, tells me. 'It's possibly the menstrual cycle.' Oh, I thought that was a ladies' bike. They say you live and learn. Well I didn't. It was my tenth day without Cold Collation.

## September 27

DIARY: SERGEANTS' MESS DANCE. RAINING

I was so excited at the prospect of UK leave that my swonicles were revolving at speed. Like a fool I thought I was going back to 1939. I'm still trying to get back to 1939. That was the best time. It all lay ahead of you. Now it's all behind and I don't want to look back. A letter from my mother tells me I have no home to come to. Her and dad are renting the ground floor of 40 Meadow Way, Woodhatch, Reigate at twenty-seven separate shillings to be paid at once to the landlady. Rations are short, they have eaten the couch. 'Your father has left the army and is working at the Associated Press in Fleet Street. If you come, you'll have to sleep in the box room on dad's officer's camp bed.' A camp bed! – a home fit for homosexuals. Brother is 'in Germany'. By order of the King of England he is hitting refugees who try to nick food.

I must hurry, Mother, for I'm to be Queen of the Ball. The Sergeants are preparing for my last trumpet solo before my leave. I must look my best for them. In my scratched steel mirror, I look lovely. It's a short walk from my room, through the Sergeant Rev. Beaton's chapel, across the connecting covered way to the Dance Hall. I'm early and I tinkle the piano. Steve Lewis is early, too – that way he avoids paying.

I'm playing a Beguine.

'Is that yours?' he says.

The song yes, the piano no.

'I've never heard you play it before.'

'I always play it before, never after.'

We had been wanting to put on a musical about British soldiers transported back to Roman times. The tune I was playing was called Roman Girl.

> You can see 'em
> At the Colosseum

> Watching their favourite gladiators
> In the arena
> There's a hyena
> Eating Christians with his friends the alligators.

There were other songs we'd prepared but owing to unforeseen circumstances, which we could not foresee coming, the show never got off the ground. Another day without Cold Collation.

The dance begins. I feel great! I sing every song, play every chorus, blow louder and longer than ever before. It was to bring about my demise, however, for watching me all the while with his beady little eyes was Brigadier Henry Woods CBE, hating every note I played. He sent up a message by Major New to tell me to 'play quieter'. I told him if they wanted a quieter trumpet player, they should indent for one, or dance further away. Fuming, the little Brigadier passed the stand with the face of an executioner. He fixed me with his 'You are for it' stare, then tripped. I laughed. It was my death sentence.

*Bdr. Milligan singing louder than has ever sung before and causing the photograph to crumble*

Note the words 'TRIUMPHED AS A VOCALIST'. Sinatra was lucky I retired early, otherwise he and his wig would never have made it.

## Hail the Chief

DIARY: OCTOBER 2

Big Parade, Bossman Cometh! Quick! hurry! no time to waste! Panic! Chaos! What's it all about? Helpppp! Field Marshall Sir Harold Alexander, GCB, CSI, DSO, MC, ADC, SAC, VWXYZ, is to inspect us. We are all drawn up in serried ranks in Alexander Barracks Square, the Great Man drives into view. Taa-raaa! Much saluting, hand-shaking, pointing, nose-picking. He is led up the steps and appears at a balcony overlooking the square. He opens his mouth to speak and a blast of thunder and ice-cold rain drown and drench him out. He is soon back in the building and from within the balcony room a voice, with a note of hysteria in it, shouts out to the now drenched troops: DISMMMMSSSSS. We all run for cover. End of parade. From the windows we watch his car fill up like a bath tub. For those who believe me not, here is an excerpt from the official version.

> The Field Mashal's car passed the guard of honour and came into the square, Sir Harold was met by Brig. J. H. Woods, C.B.E., and escorted to the platform outside the concert room windows, and then it all happened.
>
> The black clouds which had been gathering for a half-hour suddenly broke and huge rain-drops fell. It was typical of a Commander who invariably has shown the greatest consideration for his troops that he immediately directed the parade to be dismissed to shelter. The men scurried to doorways and under trees, waiting a while on the chance of still hearing the Field Marshal, but the storm was too much and he drove off

In true British Iconoclastic style, the quadrangle rang with gales of laughter. Anything that pricks the balloon of pomposity is fair game for the Anglo Saxon.

## England Home and Beauty

Yes, I was going home to England and taking my beauty with me. I sent a hasty note to Harry.

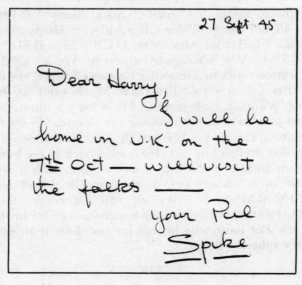

27 Sept 45

Dear Harry,

I will be home in U.K. on the 7th Oct — will visit the folks —

your Pal

Spike

## October 5

A crowd of over a hundred, some even older, are waiting at the siding. Sgt Prosser is my travelling companion. It's sunny, we are all in a holiday mood.

'Here she comes,' says Prosser looking up the line.

'And there she goes,' I say, as it goes right past.

Finally a string of Wagons-Lits clank slowly into place; a scramble of khaki porridge as we fight for seats. Len and I sink down in corner seats opposite each other. It's Sergeants only, but ah! ha!, I have added a third stripe to my sleeve. A shuddering clanking as the engine is coupled, a jerking start as the engine gets up steam; gradually we gain momentum and in ten minutes rejoin the same line in Caserta. Much points changing and shouts from the railway men, and we are set fair for Rome, a hundred miles north. Thank God I had Len for company, not one of these NCOs would talk, save for an odd grunt. 'Any minute now,' I said, 'they'll go Baaa.' They brought to this sunny day the atmosphere of a Coroner's waiting-room.

All rail journeys are identical – looking out of windows, yawning, walking up corridors, smoking, the occasional exchange of conversation, sleeping, scratching, smoking, reading. We pass through war-torn Sessa Arunca, a long tunnel through Monte de Fate, the country alternates between mountain and plain. I prefer my countryside plain, don't you? Through Minturno, the area where I had last been in action. I point out Colle Dimiano.

'That's where I was wounded,' I tell Len and the entire carriage. 'Did the Sergeant kiss it better?' says Len.

Midday, and we are on the plain approaching Cisterna, to our left the Via Appia, up into the Alban Hills dotted with white crosses from the Anzio break-out. By one o'clock we are hissing and chuffing into Rome Central Station. 'Half an hour,' shouts a voice. We debouch and stretch our legs, then taking from the vendor's trolley, stretch our teeth on sticky gooey cakes which look like noses boiled in treacle.

The platforms are scurrying with Romans, all looking like unshaven Barclays Bank managers in Cricklewood. The supply of pretty Italian girls seems endless. 'They must have a factory round here,' says Len, eating what looks like a dried mango with cockroaches stuck on it. We both agree that to eat continental pastries you should be sedated or blindfolded. A sloppy thin, violently ugly Railway Transport officer comes a-clumping and a-shouting through a bull horn: 'All Liap Pwarty number Twenty-six bwack on the twain.' We had stocked up with French bread, cheese and boiled noses in treacle plus a bottle of Chianti. The guard's shrill whistle, unlike British guards', plays arias from *Madame Butterfly*: he's still blowing when we've left the station.

We are not hungry, so we start to eat the bread and cheese right away. The prognosis is we should be in Calais at exactly 'some time tomorrow'. When I wake up the train is speeding past Lake Bracciano; at the level crossing a crowd of peasants stand with open mouths. It's getting colder. So is mine. We can see snow on distant mountains. We plunge into long dark tunnels then into bright sunlight, into Umbria and through Viterbo, once in misty yesterdays an Etruscan Citadel. We are climbing, the windows are steaming up, we turn the handle from Freddo to Caldo, and soon we are nice and Caldo. Darkness descends, dingy yellow light bulbs illuminate the carriage. Heads are nodding, time for beddy-byes. I see there's room under the seat to sleep, I squirm underneath, bliss, there's a heating pipe behind me. While the dodos sleep upright, I sleep the sleep of an angel, be it fallen.

A merry Jiminy Cricket Castrati voice is calling: 'Wake up, wake up . . . we're in Milan.' 'Bollocks' is the response. It's eight o'clock on a very dull cold morning which I see through a sea of legs and boots. The smell in the carriage is like an uncleaned chicken coop on a hot day. Rasping smokers' coughs greet the morning. Milan station stands gaunt, grey and steely cold in the early gloom. The platform is almost empty save for vendors. We drink their exquisite aromatic coffee, banging our feet, expelling steam on our breath.

'How did you sleep?' I ask.

'Sitting up, didn't you notice?'

He hasn't slept well, because he hasn't slept at all. What did he do?

'I read the *Corriere della Sera*.' He doesn't speak Iti, but when you're awake all bloody night, it's amazing what you can manage.

'All Liap Pwarty number twenty-six bwack on twain.'

He's still around! With my ablution kit I spruce up in the toilet. What the hell, why not? I strip off for a stand-up bath. The train is on a dodgy bit of track. Trying to wash one leg while standing on the other, the train lurches and one leg goes down the toilet up to the groin. It's the nutcracker suite. I exit to a queue of strained faces: 'Been 'avin' a bloody barf?' says one micturated voice. Why should I tell these rough soldiers that, quite apart from crushing my nuts, I have partaken of Italian train waters and my body is now snow white and ready for leave.

What's this? A buffet car has been added? Len and I wobble along the steamed-up corridors past the odd dozy soldier. It's very nice, bright and clean with white tablecloths and friendly waiters. Our waiter is fat and looks suspiciously like Mussolini. He smiles. We order egg and chips. He stops smiling.

The scenery is now ravishing. Cobalt-tinted lakes, blue mountains with snow caps, pine forests, cascading gorges, all displayed in bright sunshine. However, in the Sergeants' carriage, it is overcast, raining, with heavy fog. An R T O Sergeant holding a clipboard is checking our documents and counting heads. God, this is exciting, this is what got Agatha Christie going on continental train murders. 'She should have travelled Southern Railways in the rush hour,' says Len. 'That's murder *all* the bloody time.' We've come to a sudden halt. I get off the floor. A look out of the window shows gangers on the line, some shouting 'twixt engine driver and gangers. Finally shouts and a whistle blowing, we chuff chuff forward. We proceed in fits and starts, starts and fits, then farts and stits.

And lo! there was darkness on the land. It was called the Simplon Tunnel. Icy cold air squirts through the crevices in the trousers and fibrillates the Brinjalls. Soon we are out of war-torn Italy into peaceful money-mad Switzerland. Customs officers have boarded at Domodossola and are checking Passports. 'Piss Pots . . . all Piss Pots pleasea,' they are calling. Two enter our cabin. No, we are travelling on the King's Warrant and don't need Piss Pots, but wish them well in their search. The lighthearted banter and laughter between Len and myself brings facial sneers, constant nudges and silent stares of hatred from our fellow passengers. People are like that. If you don't understand them, hate them. What better species to drop the Bomb on! Alas they outnumber us.

CHEERFUL CHAPS .... 2   MISERABLE BASTARDS. 10

MISERABLE BASTARDS WIN BY                              8

The suburbs of Basle. What's this? Union Jacks hanging from the buildings and signs: 'Vive Tommy'. When the train slows, they foist apples and almond cakes on us, girls run alongside and hand us flowers. A quick look into my scratched steel mirror tells me why. I am still beautiful. I lean forward from the window to show my medal ribbons, and just in case I point to them.

Basle station is like Waterloo without the crap. We are greeted by another R T O Officer: 'L I A P party twenty-six? The train will be here for an hour. Refreshments have been laid on at the station buffet, no charge, just show your rail pass.' Despite 'no charge', they all charge to the buffet. What a lovely surprise to hear the pretty waitresses saying, 'We 'ave for you, ze Collation of Coldness.' Lovely – can they whistle the Warsaw Concerto to complete our happiness? But what a difference. Cold Collation here is different from Cold Collation in Catford. Here it's great slices of turkey, a whole lettuce, great dollops of thick egg-bound mayonnaise, chunky brown bread. And here was a moment of delight: one of the grim miserable sergeants bites the thick chunky bread, his teeth come out in it, and he goes on eating.

'So, the we'll-be-in-Calais-some-time-tomorrow isn't going to materialize,' says Len, not fancying another night of upright somnabulism.

'Can you hear horses galloping, Len?'

Len listens. 'No, I can't.'

'Oh, that's the second time today.'

He looks at me and shakes his head. 'It's time you had leave. Look, this is Switzerland, you could seek asylum here.'

Back in the compartment of miserable bastards, Len consults his map. 'We are about 450 miles to Calais.'

'Any advance on 450? Do I hear 460? Sold then to Sgt Prosser for 450.'

The Sergeants all steam with hate. I gain satisfaction from knowing that bloody ugly wives with faces like dogs' bums with hats on are waiting for them. Ha ha ha ha! It's getting still colder, but not as cold as Collation. Dinner? The white tablecloths are victims of sloppy eating and shunting. Would we like egg and chips? says Mussolini – if so you can scrape it off the table. Nay, we'll have some pasta. He has a heart attack. He runs screaming to the chef telling him of the breakthrough. I hear the kitchen staff singing hymns. Mussolini returns with steaming plates of ravioli. Tears come to his eyes as we eat it.

Night has encapsulated us, semaphores of light flash past the windows like speeding fireflies. We pause a while over our coffee and brandy and think of my parents possibly drinking watery Horlicks, eating the cat, and listening to the nine o'clock noise in rented accommodation. Was I really going back to that? Yes I was. I should have got off in Switzerland.

We return to our compartment. All the repulsive Sergeants are laughing and joking, but stop the moment we return. They smirk as we sit down and I wonder what's fretting at the smooth surface of their delinquent minds. I crawl under the seat to last night's sleeping niche and turn off to the sound of iron crochets of train wheels. While we slumber, the land of Jeanne D'Arc is slipping by in the D'ark.

## Awake, My Pretty Ones

The sun is streaming through the carriage windows. Poplar trees are flashing past, the French countryside is a swirl of autumnal hues.

'Bonjour,' says Len, as I arise from le floor. 'It's temps pour le breakfast.'

The buffet car is crammed with bleary-eyed, travel-weary soldiers. The smell of fried breakfasts wafts along the corridors; they've started queuing, we must be getting near England. Appetite improves with waiting. Our turn. What would the messieurs like? Hot bread rolls? Oui, oui. We must be in France or luck. There's *real* unsalted Normandy butter on the table. We watch it melt on the hot rolls, heap on marmalade. 'Le Life is Très Bon,' says Len. He confers with his le map. 'Ah, we passed Chaumont in the night,' he says. Help, Doctor, Doctor, I've been passing Chaumonts in the night.

We are coursing the side of the historic Marne river. To our left the verdant plain of Champagne. Blue overalled vignerons are harvesting the grapes. The train slows down into Epernay. My God! Champagne vendors on the platform! It's only ten o'clock in the morning, we'll be pissed by twelve.

'It's a giveaway,' Len said.

I waited, they didn't give it away. It was fresh and sparkling and delicious. I remember my parents telling me of their Salad Days in India during the Afternoon of the Raj. They used to drink Heidsicke Dry Monopole, and here was I twenty years on drinking it for the first time.

I was wrong, we were pissed by eleven. We buy a second bottle for the journey.

'All Liap No. 26 back on the twain.'

A late purchase of some Brie and we glide from the station. In the distance we see the exquisite Château Sarat. How can people live in such luxury, while my parents are eating the furniture. Never mind, I'll be rich one day, and if possible the day after that as well. We are at sea level, but none is getting in. What? We are *not* going to stop in Paris. This is a breach of the Geneva Convention.

'The rotten bastards,' says Len, who was looking forward to Paris, and is now looking back at it. Never mind, there'll be another war. Before that we must open the champagne! We retire to the corridor. Like barbarians we shake the living daylights out of the bottle. This was the way Clark Gable opened it in San Francisco. We swig from the bottle and soon we aren't missing Paris at all. We are jolted awake as the train suddenly screeches to a halt. Amiens. My God, we are reinforcements for World War One. 'Oh,' says Len, 'that stuff.' I didn't know he'd had a stuff, he must have done it while I was asleep.

The RTO Sergeant is wobbling down the corridors: 'Calais in two hours.' he calls. I must wash and brush up. Calais, one of the Sunk Ports.

'Have you ever seen the statue of the Burghers in Calais?' says Len.

'No, I'm waiting till they make the film.'

A last coffee in the Buffet car. The waiters are breathing a sigh that the culinary barbarians are leaving. But what bad cooks the English are – they even burnt Joan of Arc.

Still miles from Calais, yet the idiot Sergeants are getting their luggage down. Some are even standing at the door. In their tiny minds they think they'll get there quicker. Why don't they stand near a graveyard?

Our train is slowing. The canvas is grey, a spaghetti of railway lines, black industrial complexes, many of them bombed skeletons. A mess of railway sidings, rolling stock, here and there a burnt-out tanker; slower and slower and then in the middle of a sea of points, we are told, 'All out!' Waiting in the grey gloom are three RTO Sergeants, all brass, blanco and bullshit. We split into two groups. 'NCOs this way please.' (PLEASE???) We two-step over a hundred yards of tracks. NO. 4 TRANSIT CAMP says the sign, and who are we to argue. 'In here, gentlemen,' (GENTLEMEN?) The Sergeant shows us into a Nissen hut. Beds and an iron stove.

'Make yourselves comfortable,' he says.

'How?' I say.

We are to report to the Camp Office for documentation. 'It says here you're a bombardier,' says a clerk.

'Yes, I'm a bombardier.'

'You've got sergeant's stripes on.'

'Yes.'

'Why?'

'It's a tertiary appointment awaiting ratification through G5 Documentation.' That floored him. He stamped my Travel Warrant and we were free from the tyranny of twits.

*The Hôtel de Ville – Where British Tea and Buns held sway that Golden October day*

101 . CALAIS . *L'Hôtel de Ville*

Well, you see the postcard. Well, it's much bigger in fact. A walk through the streets of Calais wasn't exactly enervating, grey; rather like Catford on a good day. The Hôtel de Ville is now Le NAAFI. We have le tea and le beans on le toast. I keep an eye open for any lads from le 19 Battery, it would be nice to see Driver Kidgell or Gunner Edgington; but no, 19 Battery are all in Holland and at this moment possibly all knee trembling in doorways. We finish le meal and partons pour le Camp. Army or not, bed is lovely, even though it's made of wood with springs missing. A goodnight gesture as Len stokes up the fire. As I doze off, I hear rain falling. It will do le garden good.

## LAST LEG OF THE JOURNEY ...

REVEILLE...... 0600

BREAKFAST .... 0700

PARADE........ 0830

EMBARK ....... 0900–1000

It all sounds reasonable, no need to see a solicitor after all. The channel steamer SS *Appalling* (the name of the ship has been changed to protect the innocent) is waiting. A tiny almost unnoticeable sign says LIAP PARTY NO. 26 ASSEMBLE HERE. We'll never do it, it's much too small to stand on. We move slowly up the gangplank like shuffling penguins. I'm humping a kitbag, big pack and trumpet case. The kitbag is vital, it contains all the hoarded underwear that my mother has promised will put me on the road to success in civvy street. And I will never be taken short. The officers in first class look down at our huddled mass from the top deck. 'There's one thing we've got over them, Len, we can see right up their noses.' A clatter of donkey engines and French steam; hawsers plummet into the waters. Cries of yo, ho, ho, and the ship slips from the quay into the muddy waters of Calais harbour, but soon we are free from the muddy French waters and out into the pure English Channel and its muddy waters. It's very choppy; ere long the first victims are starting to retch. Whereas other ranks are seasick, officers only have Mal-de-Mer, as befits the King's commission. Sleek white gulls glide alongside. In their total freedom, we must look like a bunch of caged monkeys. It's getting rougher; three green men are throwing up at the rail. Thank God for gravity.

## Landlords Ahoy!

Frightening Folkestone on the Kardboard Kow! The golden seaport hove into view; I would rather have viewed into Hove. It's raining, and doing the gardens good. We are close to the quay.

'It looks so bloody foreboding,' Len says. 'I think I'll go back.'

I remind him that his dear little wife is at this moment panting on her bed with the heating turned up and drinking boiling Horlicks.

The customs are pretty hot. 'Read that, please.' I am handed a foolscap sheet of writing.

'Very good,' I say.

'Have you anything to declare?'

I declare that the war is over. He's not satisfied. What have I got in the case. It's a trumpet. Can he see it. He opens the case. Where did I buy this? In London. Have I got a receipt? Yes. Where is it? It's in an envelope in a drawer in my mother's dressing-table in Reigate.

He hums and haws, he's as stupid as a pissed parrot. 'Empty your kitbag.' I pour out a sea of my second-hand underwear. He turns it over and over. 'Where is it?'

'Where's what?'

'The contents.' He thinks it's the wrapping for something. Why have I got so many underpants? I tell him of my mother's forecast of the coming world shortage that will hit England soon. He is now pretty pissed off. OK. He makes a yellow chalk mark on everything. Next to me he finds a poor squaddie with a bottle of whisky. 'You'll have to pay One Pound Ten Shillings on that,' he says with malice aforethought.

'Oh no I won't,' says the squaddie.

'Than I'll have to confiscate it.'

The squaddie opens the bottle and hands it round to us. With devilish glee we help lower the level to halfway, then the squaddie puts the bottle to his lips and drains it. The customs officer is in a frenzy, says to an M P, 'Arrest that man.'

The M P wants to know why.

'Drunkenness,' he says.

'He's not drunk,' says the M P.

'Wait,' says the customs officer.

From the quay to the station, we are now free of military encumbrances. Just for the hell of it we go into a little teashop in the high road. It's very quiet. Three middle-aged ladies are serving.

'Tea, love?' says one in black with a little white apron.

'Yes, tea love.' That, and a slice of fruit cake that tastes like sawdust. The sugar is rationed to two lumps. The war isn't quite over yet. We pay tenpence. Folkestone station and the 11.40 train to Charing Cross. London is as I left it – black, grimy, rainy but holes in the terraces where bombs have fallen. Len and I split.

'See you in four weeks' time, two stone lighter and skint,' he says.

I buy my first English newspapers for two years. The *Daily Herald*, the *Daily Mail*, the *Express*, the *Mirror*, the *News Chronicle*. I go straight for my beloved Beachcomber and find that Justice Cocklecarrot and the Red Bearded Dwarfs are still in court. He is sentencing a Mrs Grotts for repeatedly pushing the Dwarfs into people's halls.

From Charing Cross I take the tube to Archway. Soon I am knocking on the door of 31 St John's Way. A surprise for Mrs Edgington, she doesn't know I'm coming.

'Oh Spike,' she's drying her hands. 'What are you doing here?'

I tell her I'm doing leave here.

'When are you going back?'

171

Can I come in first? Tea, would I like some tea. Ah! at last an *English* cup of tea and a dog biscuit. (JOKE) I explain my accommodation difficulty. What is the difficulty? Accommodation. Yes, I can stay here. 'You can sleep in the basement.' Mr Edgington's not in, he's gone out to get a paper. Yes, he's well. Son Doug? He's been called up. The Army. Did I know Harry was getting married on leave? He's been caught at the customs with some material he'd bought for Peg's wedding dress and the bastards have given him detention. Mr Edgington is back. Ah Spike. 'When are you going back?' He's tall, thin, at one-time handsome. An ex-Guards Sergeant from World War One, he was badly gassed in France. He is in receipt of a small war pension. Alas he smokes, it will do for him one day, as it would his youngest son Doug . . . I dump my gear in the basement. Would I like some lunch? Toad-in-the-hole? Lovely grub. I set myself up in the basement. There's a coal fire, but remember it's rationed! Best not light it until the evening.

Leading question. Can Mrs Edgington see to find room for Sergeant Betty Cranley for a day or so? Yes, there's Doug's bedroom going spare. I tell her, good, because I'm going spare. I phone Betty: Hello Betty, knickers and boobs, can she get up with knickers and boobs this week knickers and boobs? Yes, she can, knickers and boobs.

'Mrs Edgington, can I have egg and chips for tea?' I light the coal fire. Mrs Edgington has lent me Doug's 'wireless', a little Bakelite Echo set. These were the days of quiet broadcasting – Christopher Stone playing gramophone records in steady measured tones, unlike the plastic arse-screaming hyped-up disc jockeys with crappy jokes, who get housewives so hyped up with fast mindless chatter and ghetto-blasting records that they are all on Valium. I spent the afternoon reading the papers and listening to long-forgotten programmes. Sid Dean and his band are broadcasting live from a tea dance in Brighton. How very very nice. The News! Alvar Liddell, ace broadcaster and Master of Wireless is telling us in profound adenoidal tones that Mr Attlee, the Prime Monster, with all the impact of sponge on marble, is meeting with the Soviet Ambassador, where they are promising each other there will never be another war, and babies are found under bushes. Churchill is at home in Chartwell doing the kitchen. Henry Hall has been in a car crash in the key of E flat. Woman's Hour: how to knit socks under water, and hints on how to make the best of rationed food (eat it).

I am staring into the glowing coals, sometimes I stare into the glowing wallpaper or the glowing lino. I decide to take my legs for a walk before supper. Do I want the door key? It's where no burglar can find it, on a string in the letter-box. I'm wearing my red and blue Artillery forage cap. In the London gloom it looks like my head's on fire. I stroll to the Archway and its grumbling grey traffic. The evening is lit with those ghastly green sodium lights that make the English look like a race of seasick Draculas. Down Holloway Road, remembering that it was down here Edward Lear was born. I stop to see what the shops have to offer. Displays of crappy furniture, boasting that you can see the 'natural grain of the cardboard'. I go down to the Seven Sisters Road. None of the sisters show up, so I come back. I pass Hercules Street, with not a person in it weighing more than ten stone. Manor Garden, Alexander Road, Landseer Road; the last two would turn in their graves to see what the names had been used for. Giesbach Road? Who chooses them? What grey, dull, mindless idiots sit and debate these improbable street names, streets that should be called Grotty Road, Dog Shit Street, Crappy Avenue, Terrible Building Road, Who-in-their-right-mind-built-these-Mansions. Mind you, it's got worse since. Ah! this is better. The fish and chip shop. A cheery fat sweating man with six hairs serves me. 'Three pieces of rock salmon and a penn'orth o'chips.' He sees my medal ribbons.

''ello son, you bin in trouble?'

Yes, I said, and her father's after me.

Back at number thirty, I pull the string on the key.

'Is that you Spike?' Mrs Edgington in her nightie, calls from the top of the stairs.

'Yes, would you like some fish and chips?' No, they've had their supper. Remember to bolt the door, but not the food. I say OK.

'If you want a cup of tea it's all there.' Ta. It's 8 o'clock. They go to bed early to save electricity and heating. It's not been an easy war for the working classes. I lie in bed eating fish and chips and sipping tea. The fire glows on to the walls. Geraldo and his band are sparkling on the radio, and Dorothy Carless is Thanking her dear for that lovely weekend, reminding me I myself have a very weak end.

Hitler is dead, and I am alive. I cannot understand it. He had so much going for him. Like the Red Army. I fall asleep to the glow of the dying fire, or am I dying to fire by the glow of sleep? It all depends on the size.

## Leave: Day 1

I awake to the sound of buses. I can tell by the tyres on wet streets. It's raining. I am wearing my new pyjamas, made from sheets by a Maddaloni tailor and dyed by the local laundry. I thought they would match my eyes.

'You awake, Spike?' Mrs Edgington at the door. 'Cup of tea.' She screams! 'What's the matter with your face, Spike?'

I say 'Everything. Why?'

'You've got blue all over it.' Does it match my eyes? Yes. It's off my bloody pyjamas. It's all over my body, now my body matches my eyes, and my eyes match the sheets. I spend the morning washing Mrs E's sheets, and finally get it off my body with a loofah. I boil the pyjamas in the copper and now they look like an old Variety backdrop for G. H. Elliot's act.

Porridge? Yes, Mrs Edgington.

'Harry loves porridge. I always gave it to the boys before they went to work. It's very good for you, gives you a good lining to your stomach.'

Mr Edgington had had his breakfast earlier. 'I'm an early riser, as soon as my eyes are open I have to get up.' He's so right, it's silly to get up with your eyes closed.

Down in the basement I tidy up, and something that is never done, I tidy down and sideways – it's silly to miss those areas. I polish my boots and my appalling brown bulging civvy shoes that weigh eighteen pounds each.

The doorbell. 'It's Betty,' said Mrs E.

'No it isn't, it's the door bell.'

There she is in her smart WAAF uniform, bright brass buttons, her WAAF mascara and WAAF lipstick. Has she brought her knickers and boobs? From the right, number one! two! We all sit round the Edgingtons' kitchen table and have 'a nice cup of tea'. Mrs E tells of the bombin', the doodle bugs, the incendries, and that married woman over the road. I'll take Betty up to the West End. There's Variety at the Met Edgware Road. Max Miller and the wonderful Wilson, Keppel and Betty. No words can describe the atmosphere of that bygone age that started in 1850 and died in the 1950s. Betty and I are in the front row. Max spots me. ''Ello son, we got a soldier 'ere back from the war? That the wife? On leave are you? Wot are you doin' 'ere then?' It's Lyons Corner House beans on toast.

Back home. 'That you Spike?' Yes. 'Don't forget to bolt the door.' Betty and I go down to the basement. Max Miller was right . . . what were we doing there?

I awake at Mrs Edgington bringing me in tea. 'Bet is in the kitchen. Did you have a nice time in London?' Yes.

Betty has to return to duty; her knickers and knockers are leaving at midday. I see her to the tube, we'll meet for further things later. She is swallowed up by the descending stairs.

## The Great Amnesia

I have a diary. It says: Stayed Edgingtons. Stayed Beryl. Stayed Folks. But I can't remember – so I searched for Beryl – Success – I found Beryl – she remembered, but won't charge me.

## Gunner Milligan Traces Beryl Southby
## Now Mrs Smith!

Yes! 40 years on! I managed to get her on the phone. Did she remember me? Yes, I'd never stopped molesting her.

ME:       Beryl, did I see you when I came on leave?
BERYL:   Yes.
ME:       Did I come and stay at your place?
BERYL:   Yes.
ME:       Oh. Er, what did we do?
BERYL:   You came and stayed with me and my mum and dad at Anerley.
ME:       What did we do?
BERYL:   (*laughing*) Don't you remember?
ME:       No, my mind's a blank.
BERYL:   Well you stayed with us, and we sort of went various places.
ME:       Where?
BERYL:   Well, I was singing at the Ballroom in Anerley and you came and saw me.
ME:       Did we go up to London?
BERYL:   Yes, you took me to the pictures in Leicester Square.
ME:       Did I take you anywhere to eat?
BERYL:   Yes, we went to the Corner House.
ME:       How long did I stay with you?
BERYL:   About a week or ten days.
ME:       Did I tell you I was coming on leave?
BERYL:   No, you devil, you never told anybody when you were arriving or leaving. The day you arrived I was with my dad, you know I was a bit of a tomboy, well, I was in the garage helping dad under a car. I was covered in grease, I looked terrible.
ME:       Nonsense, you are a very pretty girl.
BERYL:   No I'm not.
ME:       No, no, you weren't pretty. You were better, you

were *different*. You always reminded me of the girls in Walt Disney full-length cartoons.

BERYL: I remember you took me to see a bloke in Streatham.

ME: That was Jack Blanks . . . he was a drummer.

BERYL: It was a road off Streatham High Street.

ME: Yes, that was Jack Blanks, he was a drummer . . . I remember I went to a dance where he was playing. I know someone was with me. Was it you?

BERYL: It could have been. I remember you went to Chappell's.

ME: Great, yes, I went to buy a trumpet.

BERYL: Yes, you were playing this trumpet in the shop and the manager asked you if you would go downstairs and try it.

ME: Yes, I was buying one for the band. I also bought some mutes and an aluminium hat mute.

BERYL: You went downstairs and you went on playing the trumpet and the manager came down again and asked if you could put a mute in as you were deafening the customers.

ME: What else?

BERYL: We went for a picnic. I had a gang of friends. You remember? Remember Curly, my sister?

ME: Yes, she was very cockney.

BERYL: That's right. She was there and my friend Irene. We went by bus and you hung a beer bottle out of the window on a string. You had the conductor in fits of laughter.

ME: What kind of person was I? I can't remember.

BERYL: You were a very nice young man, you were always smiling, and you always wanted to do something different from anybody else.

I daren't ask her if I'd showed her my post-war reserve underwear. As Beryl spoke, it all came back. I remember the

Corner House if only for the three-string orchestra, still lost in the 1900s, ploughing into Fritz Kreisler's repertoire while I ate scrambled egg on toast. Beryl didn't know what terrible danger she was in. We sat at night and listened to Harry Parry and the Radio Rhythm Club with Benny Lee. I also remember now that her mother made sensational roast beef and Yorkshire pudding for a Sunday lunch. I now know that I was, in my mind, living a dream life. I was floating on other people's emotions, and only concerned with my own which were very childlike, naïve, and basically, deep down, there was a yearning for recognition. Recognition of what is not clear, but I know there was some goal in my life to be fulfilled. Sometimes I thought it might be as a painter, but mostly it was as a musician, maybe as a composer. None of these materialized, except in a minor capacity.

Beryl and I also made a flying visit to see my parents. She says my father answered the door and said 'What do you want?'

I said, 'Don't you remember me? I'm your son.'

'Ah yes.' He called, 'Kiddie,' (my mother) 'come and see who it is.'

My mother came out, drying her hands and said, 'Oh son, I had a premonition you were coming, I've just baked a nice ginger cake.'

I didn't stay that night. Having found out where they lived and seen that they recognized me as their son and a ginger-cake eater, I returned for the last but one week.

And so to that occasion. A third-class from Charing Cross to Reigate. How nice was the buttoned upholstery of the compartments on the old Southern Railway. I've a carriage to myself and I settle back with the *Daily Herald*. It's a sunny day; my eyes wander from the paper to the window. Lewisham Junction – and 'the Government are to increase the sugar ration' as we speed through Catford. By Sydenham, 'Burnley have drawn with Queens Park Rangers after extra time'; as we pass the Crystal Palace Towers, 'Mr Attlee is saying that demobilization is to be speeded up' at Croydon. An old couple get on. They reek of Sanatogen. 'Young man, does this train go to Reigate?' Yes it does, 'and Mr Attlee went on to say that there will be jobs for all returning soldiers' and 'Tickets, please, all tickets please' says an Inspector. I show him my rail warrant. 'On leave son?' he says, cutting a V in the document. He has a son in France as Purley Junction flashes past. He's in the Marine Commandos. Yes, madame, it definitely goes to Reigate. The Inspector leaves, his steel clippers mincing in his hand, hungry for tickets. The old couple sit close together. He is thin and bald, and when she takes her hat off, so is she. They are worried about Reigate. Does it go there? Yes it does! Yes, yes, I'm sure Mr Attlee is going to Reigate. 'He says all war criminals will be sentenced to Reigate.' Reigate Grand Station, and we get off on to the deserted platform. 'Is this Reigate, young man?' Yes, this is Reigate young man. With kitbag, pack and trumpet case I catch the Green Line bus that drops me at the bottom of the hill. I gasp and stagger upwards. Betty, oh Betty, what did you do to my manhood?

A car stops. 'Want a lift, Sergeant?' A moustachioed Major with a face like a dismantled sink pump.

'Yes sir,' providing he doesn't want to rattle me knackers.

'On leave?'

'Yes sir, from Italy.'

'Oh, you missed all the bombin'.'

'No, I've never missed the bombin'. Ha ha ha ha ha hooray Henry.' He drops me at the very gate. 40 Meadow Way, Woodhatch.

'Thank you very much sir,' and if I ever see you again, it'll be two weeks too soon.

I turn to see my mother's white face at the parlour window, looking for scandal. I see her mouth the words 'Oh, it's Terry' and appear at the door. 'My son . . . My son.' Good, she remembers me! 'You came back, despite the ginger cake,' she says. 'When are you going back?' Can I come in? Would I like some tea? 'Oh my son, my son.' Good, she still remembers me. 'Your telegram said today or tomorrow.' Yes, so I've come today, but yesterday, today *was* tomorrow, so what's the problem? The 6×4 box room is all ready for you. A single bed with a pink eiderdown, a steel cream painted fireplace blocked with newspaper, a bedside table with barley twist legs, a po, a dressing-table with a cracked mirror, a cane chair painted silver, a standard lamp with an oil cloth shade with pirate ships on it. A ceiling light with a white globe. There are no windows. 'It's the best we could do, son.' She hugs me again. What a memory she has.

But wait, where is my father, Captain Leo A. Milligan R A R A O C Retired? Why wasn't he standing at the gates with the Irish wolfhounds on a leash, his saffron kilt blowing in the Reigate winds, his piper at his elbow playing 'Danny Boy', and holding out the traditional bannock.

'What are you talking about, my son, has the war done this to you?' Of course, he's at work, I forgot.

I hang up my clothes in the cupboard. In one corner is my poor brother's pre-war suit – you can see the coat hanger through it. There's his shirts, his Marks and Spencer's flannels and his sports jacket which must have been dead a year.

Would I like some tea and fruit cake? She's made the fruit cake special, because 'You've always liked it.' Wrong, fruit cake gives me the shits. We have it on a tray in the front room. 'It gets the sun in the afternoon.' Mum is looking well, she is fifty, she's survived three crowned heads, seven crowned bodies and eighteen cats. Brother Desmond? He's fine, he's in the Ox and Bucks. How thrilling. He's stationed in Hamburg, and has piles. He writes regularly, boringly, but regularly. His letters say, 'Can you please not send me any more fruit cake?' I asked her why Dad left the army. 'His old firm Associated Press and Slavery wanted him back as soon as possible to work him like a nigger' at 7 pounds a week. In doing so he had lost thousands of pounds. He would have had to do one more week in the army to qualify for an officer's pension, but then he was Irish: a nation of people given to leaving the army one week early. Mum has to go and get dinner ready. I'm left to the wireless and those books from my boyhood, now on foreign shelves. Music While You Work is fighting to escape from our one-valve wireless. I put my feet up and blow the Players cigarette smoke into the air, helping to foul the room, darken the ceiling and prepare my parents for lung cancer. Though I can't see the hole, I'm bored, I need action! I leap to my feet and walk briskly to the fireplace. No, it isn't enough, I still need action, so I walk briskly back again to the couch. Outside it has been, as father said, a 'Golden Autumn day'.

By the time he returns it is a dark rainy night and he's been working like a nigger. I welcome him home dripping wet and shagged out. My dear dad, home from the office, home from the wars, home one week too soon for his officer's pension. He was something special, both clown and romantic, kind and gentle. He smiles that smile which twists halfway up the side of his face, showing his huge teeth with the gold filling.

'Ah my son, my son,' he says. So he remembers me too. 'Well, well, son, home at last eh?' Yes, I'm home at last eh. It's amazing that after two years away we don't have anything to communicate. After 'how are you keeping', I ask him how *he* is keeping. He says 'Fine, fine,' and I say 'Fine, fine.' Well, well, home from the wars eh, son? Well, well, yes, and I'm fine, well, well, my son home from the war. When mother comes into the room it becomes '*our* son home from the war'. I save the presents until after dinner. 'Thanks son,' says Dad, lighting up an Edward the 7th cigar, while my mother clutches rosary-blessed-by-the-Pope-number-sixty-seven. My Father: 'Must hear the nine o'clock news.' He's just come from bloody *Fleet Street* and he wants to hear the news! Would I like a sherry? We all make a little toast, they to my homecoming, and me to the man who assassinates the vintner that markets the sherry. It's like rat's piss. So, sipping my rat's piss, we talk about the empty years between. 'The Associated Press are working me to death,' he says. If that is true they should pay him more. 'The Americans work the British like niggers. And that is the end of the nine o'clock news.' Dad and Mum retire. He has to get up early to be worked to death like a nigger.

It's too early for me. There's nothing wrong with Reigate,

*Father working at A.P.*

there's always the streets. 'There's a nice pub over the Green,' says Mum. OK. The key is on a string in the letterbox. Don't be late and ruin your health. Yes, The Bell, I'll go there for a drink. You never know. It's full of stockbrokers, and what appears to be a Morticians' Convention. I alone am in uniform. The medals do it. Was I in the Invasion, son? Yes, I was killed the first day. What will I have? A whisky and a blindfold. They won't let me buy a round. I am really quite a nice young man. What's that decoration? That's Mentioned in Despatches. Why? I don't know, someone just mentioned me in despatches. Sometimes they mentioned me in the canteen, sometimes in passing, sometimes in the Naafi, on this occasion in despatches. Time gentlemen please!

I walk out and smell that damp autumn musk. It's misty and cool. I make my fun-loving way across the Green to 40 Meadow Way.

'Is that you son?' Yes Mum. 'Have you ruined your

health?' No mum. 'If you're hungry there's plenty of bread and cheese in Sainsbury's in the High Street.' I hear my father snoring, plaster falls from the ceiling. 40 Meadow Way, Woodhatch, is not for the faint of heart. I sleep soundly, and in great purity.

## Dawn Over Reigate and 40 Meadow Way

Father has left at some unearthly hour to work like a nigger. Mother tells me he had a good breakfast. 'Porridge, it gives a good lining to your stomach,' eat it all up son, it will do you good. I bet you missed your mother's cooking, didn't you son. Now, have I any dirty washing? She's doing a boil today. Yes. I proudly show her my collection of post-war underwear. 'What are they son – floor cloths?' She boils them. Several disintegrate and float to the surface as froth, some survive but die later that night.

A lazy day, endless cups of tea, smoking. 'You'll ruin your health, son.' Fruit cake, the shits, and Primo Scala and his Accordion Band on Workers' Playtime. How can people work with that noise? Twenty accordions playing those digital dysentery numbers with thousands of notes spewing out to show off their technique. Monte Ray sings in a strangled nasal castrati voice. The afternoon turns into evening.

I nip out to telephone Betty Cranley and her body. She's booked a room at the Admiral Owen Inn in Sandwich as Mr and Mrs Cranley. Can she buy a cheap ring to make it look official? Why not? Would she like me to wear a top hat and hurl confetti in the receptionist's face? Don't be a silly sod. She says we can go for long walks. What *is* she talking about? I replace the melted phone and get dressed again.

'Is that you son?' Yes, it's that me son. 'Wipe your feet, it's very muddy outside.' More tea, fruit cake and the shits. It's dark now. My mother is saving electricity; she's cooking in braille in a blacked-out kitchen. Footsteps on the path and Red Indian war dance stamping. It's my father's shaking-the-mud-off ritual.

'Is that you kid?' says Mother. She thinks he's a goat. Dad comes in shagged out from working like a nigger. We'll have to move nearer into London, the journey is killing him. How terrible, first his firm now the journey. When am I going back? He takes his shoes off his Fleet Street weary feet. His shoes are going home, this hole is letting the rain in, and this one lets it out again. He can't understand it, they cost twelve shillings and they're only thirty years old. I cheer him up, I have brought him a nice bottle of Tokay. He likes Tokay: it speaks of gypsies and caravans in the woods with leaping bonfires and bare-shouldered girls. Supper is boiled hake. He sips the Tokay appreciatively.

'Ah, a fine wine, made by bare-shouldered gypsy girls leaping over bonfires.'

When am I going back? I must leave them on the morrow, I'm to be married in Sandwich. What am I talking about? You be careful in Sandwich, they warn, it'll ruin your health. Father must hear the nine o'clock noise. We all sit facing the fretwork front of the battery set. We twiddle (yes twiddle) the knobs and home in on Alvar Liddell. Coal production is up! Quick, open the champagne. Ernie Bevin has piles and is going in for the operation. There's trouble in Palestine, there's trouble in Indo China, there's trouble in 40 Meadow Way, Reigate, the lights have fused. My father is in the broom cupboard. Who made these bloody silly fuses? Ah, he's done it. He screams as 240 volts flow through him, through the house and onto his quarterly bill, and that is the end of the news.

I spend a few more days with them. Every night my Father returns from the Associated Press, looking more and more like a nigger. In the evenings we talk about the future. I say I don't think there is one, this is really life after death. How can a nice Catholic boy say that? No, I must return to the Woolwich Arsenal dockyard and work hard and wait for promotion or death. I tell them that my workshop at Woolwich Arsenal is now a giant bomb crater. Quick, the nine o'clock news, hurry. Coal production is now going sideways. Ernie Bevin has had his operation and I'm going to sleep. 'There's a po by the bed, son.'

## Saucy Sandwich

The train to Sandwich takes me through the Kent countryside. All is russet with pale gold sunshine glistening on autumn-damp trees; through the Kent orchards, the trees heavy with the red green and yellow fruit. 1930s men are up splayed apple-ladders taking in the harvest. The curving line loops round Sandwich bay to the little station. There, not waiting for me, is Betty Cranley. The little cow!

I fiddle my way into town and get to the RAF depot. Like Simon Legree I burst into the kitchen and catch her. She's rolling dough for a pudding. So this is how you treat me. While I'm on the platform being lovely, you're rolling dough for puddens. She's sorry, she was put on duty owing to one of the staff being taken suddenly something or other. Would I like a cup of tea and some fruit cake? How nice. Does she know 'Lae thar piss tub darn bab'? I hang around until she comes off duty. It wasn't easy in an RAF kitchen full of WAAFS, all in the prime of cooking puddens.

She's gone to tart up, and reappears radiant in her skyblue uniform, buttons blazing, all smart and ready to be married in the Admiral Owen. What a dirty little devil I was. I am about to be led astray by this naughty girl. What's this, two Sergeants sleeping together? What does KRs say about this. We don't care. We sign the register before a cow of a landlady with that 'we know what you're going to do' look. What time would we like calling. I say December.

It was hell, folks. Betty threw me on to the bed and had her way with me. She used cold compresses, it was no good, I was getting weaker and weaker. I tell her I've got a headache. She can cure it she says, jumping up and down in a fever of sweat and pudding. In the morning she is bubbling with life, as I lay like a geriatric on my death bed, white and feeble. I must get to some Eggs and Chips soon, or a monastery. By day I lay in bed dreading the nights. She returns, strips off, and standing on the bed head, dives on me. When the woman comes to make the bed, she doesn't notice I'm in it. Twice she puts me in the laundry basket. Oh thank God, it's time to go back to Italy, dear. This is our last night, she says, we must make it last. She makes it last, I don't. I slept through the last bit.

*The Admiral Owen – where I aged 30 years in a night. The room of naughtiness is marked with an X.*

Morning has broken, and so have I. It's goodbye! She helps me dress. I am on the platform, a cold wind blowing through the seams of my trousers. Will I write to her. Yes. Soon? Yes, I'll start right away. She can hear the train coming, have we time for a quickie? No. The guard helps me on the train. Am I her Grandfather? The train pulls out. I wave, and she is soon lost to view. I must rest and get my strength back so that I can get off the train unaided. It's eighteen miles to Frisky Folkestone, the sun is setting, and so am I. I'm ruining my health.

## Folkestone

I report to a huge requisitioned transit hotel on the sea front, stripped of everything except the floor. I report to the Orderly Sergeant, check documents, yes the boat leaves at 0900. Bunk beds to infinity, one dull light bulb illuminates the gloom. The room gradually fills with leave-spent soldiers. Here is the historic handwritten record of those exciting days in Funny Folkestone:

*A day in Folkestone*

The Channel crossings in winter are not
    what could be called invigorating – this
    becomes even more obvious when returning
    from Leap 25 – Folkstone at 1.30 a.m., cold,
    rain (also cold), — , dim, and 1000 troops,
    all feeling rather annoyed about 'going
    back' blooms into an atmosphere of gloom –
    – "S – it" S thinks to meself – and decided
    to go sick in the morning, thereby missing
    the morning boat which pulls out at 0930hr.
    At 5 o'clock the loud speakers gently break
    the news that its Reveille – and breakfast
    is "on the table" – S arise, comb my hair,
    and consider that  enough for my morning
    toilette – Sheep like  join the long
    miserable  queue – a cigarette tastes
    like damp twigs so S extinguish the bloody
    thing — much waiting, shuffling thru corridor
    passages + up flight of wooden stairs, yellow bulbs
    gine of their cheerful 2 volt? brilliance —
    40 minutes of this saw us with a plate of

porridge + in lovely sausage + mash, naturally the tea is <u>the</u> pièce de resistance, straight back to bed, ~~the rest of the bar~~ as I would not be needed at the MT Room until 9.30 – the rest moved out at 6 ~~30~~, 5 <sup>by 8.30</sup> the whole building was empty bar a few 'Static staff' as they were called. ~~(as)~~ (on considering the word 'Static' I found it would be applicable to this particular Staff) It was strangely quiet after all the noise of departing boots —— My attempt to go sick gained me one days respite — simply because there was no more ~~ships~~ ships (I call them ships – but if they were 10 ft shorter they would be called rafts). — I phoned up Cpl. Betty Grayson and the sweet little girl said she'd be down (after getting over the first shock I knowing I was still in camp (etc.) — I waited at a ~~nother~~ sort of meal NAAFI for her to arrive – I consumed 20 wads and 2 Gallons of tea played 30 odd times

on the piano before the 'Lady in Blue'
arrived — we fell into each others
eyes on meeting — and passed the time
away at a pub, pic, + restaurant — about
10 o'clock we set off to the Station, and
held hands till the train arrived — the
feeling of sadness invades the strongest heart
and mine is most strong. — I watch the
little white face disappear
into the dust air + darkness, watched it
until the whole train looked like a string
of electric bubbles racing along into the night
I walked back along the lonely
streets to the Transit Hotel — it was still
empty — and I fell asleep hearing the thought
of 5 o'clock reveille — . But 5 o'clock was
all that — away to the boat in the chopping
rain — I linked up with another guy from
Echelon and we embarked together — we were
on the deck below main deck and
amplifiers told us about the precautions everything

except "please adjust your dress before leaving" —
the ship rolled and I land on the floor —
and slept — I was awakened by my companion
telling me of we were as good as in the
clutches of Calais — we disembarked on
a maze of railway lines and after following
the leader of the herd arrived at
the well missened '4 Transit Camp — we had
our money changed, cards issued, tickets
stamped drew Naffi — free issue and paid
out 5/= in francs (50Fr.) in case we wanted
to visit the Town — after a wash and shave
with cold water in a tin bowl, we set
out to "do" Calais — after questioning
our way — we arrived at a large
Red Brick the Town Municipal Building
done in Red brick, with white stone
trimmings — the tower of this appeared
to be top heavy at the —

191

The YMCA was situated in the Square —
and the interior of it was medieval France
almost akin to our Tudor style — a large
Dinner Hall stairs at the far end leading
to a balcony — it had an athmesphere and
that which counts in a building, theres no
denying — the continent has something — either
you feel it, or you dont — I do.

What a filler! I knew it would come in useful one day.

On board the steam packet, we pitch and toss on the grey spume-flecked waters, heading into a chill wind, laced with face-pecking rain. Some walk around the decks, I stay in what in better days was the saloon dining-room. Now it's just tables, chairs, tea, buns and fag ends. The eyes blink, the mind goes into neutral, the throb of the ship's engines. It's rather like taking a boat to the Styx. Alas, it's worse, soon it's Crappy Calais and the excitement of No. 4 Transit Camp with its damp beds and go-as-you-please urinal. A visit to the Hotel de Ville. Beans on toast cooked by a French chef made our journey a little more bearable.

Strange I never mentioned my travelling companion's name; and from what I remember, I'm glad. Next morning it's raining in French. It will do le garden bon. I'm glad to be on the train heading for Italy. The leave was an experience – it was like a flashback to 1940, and trying to compress it all into four weeks. We leave the dripping eaves of Calais, through its still slumbering populace. It's only seven-thirty and dark. My God, it's those Sergeants. They're all sitting opposite me again. And I don't have Len Prosser to talk to – he's on the train ahead.

# RETURN TO ITALY

## Return to Italy

The morning of November the second dawns. A hurrying
R T O Sergeant proceeds down the corridor. 'Maddaloni in
fifteen minutes.' Familiar landscape is in view, the hills
behind Caserta are light and dark in the morning sun. We
wipe the steamed windows to see it. I've had breakfast: two
boiled eggs, boiled bread and boiled tea. How come the
Continentals can't make tea? If this is tea, bring me coffee. If
this is coffee, bring me tea. The Italian waiter says they
don't go much on tea. I tell him if they did it would make it
stronger. The black giant locomotive groans and hisses to a
clanking steaming halt, there's a long shuddering final hiss
as the steam leaches out, like a giant carthorse about to die.
We all climb down on to the tracks. A few thank the unshaven smoke-blackened driver. There's a clutch of lorries
waiting, they are dead on time. Now the war's over the
Army's getting it together. Wearily we clamber on board
and arrive at Alexander barracks as the town is coming to
life. Shagged-out cats are heading for home and the odd
early morning dog sits on the cold pavement, freezing his
bum and scratching away the night fleas.

'Wake up, Steve.' I shake the sleeping Yew. 'Wake up, God's
in his heaven, all's right with the world.'
    'Piss off,' he says, without opening his eyes.
    'Wake up Steve my old friend, it's me, Sunny Spike Mil-
ligan, back from foreign shores with a tale to tell.'
    He raises his lovely head, squints, groans, and lets his head
fall back with a thud. Go away Milligan, go a long way
away, take a known poison and only come back when you're
dead.
    I take his eating irons and bring him his breakfast. This
thaws him out.
    'Breakfast in bed,' he says, sitting up, pulling strings that
raise the mosquito net, empty the po, release his shirt, loosen
his pyjamas, bring his socks, raise his vest, lower his comb,
push his boots . . . So what was England like? It's like 1939

with bomb craters and fruit cake, and there's a lot of it about. I should know, I'm just recovering. Back into the office grind. What news? During the absence of the band on leave, entertainment has come to a halt.

## Redivivus

'We've got to do a spot on the Variety Bill this Monday.' Stan Britton welcomes me back. 'They want something funny and musical.' How about 'Ave Maria' naked in gumboots filled with custard? No? Then 'Your Tiny Hand Is Frozen' sung from inside a fridge through the keyhole. No? Why am I wasting my time on this man when I could be wasting it on a woman in Sandwich?

## Shock Horror Etc and Other Headlines!

I was to get the chop! Not the leg of lamb or the kidney but the chop! While I was helping the women of England get back to normal in Sandwich, Brigadier Henry Woods has decided that either I go or he stays.

BOMBARDIER MILLIGAN S. 954024

With effect from November the umpteenth,
the above will be posted to the CPA,
Welfare Department, Naples.

Signed H Woods, Brigadier and midget.

So, he was the coloured gentleman in the wood pile. I swore I would never go to the pictures with him again. (He died a few years ago. I wish him well.) Why was he persecuting me like this? My only crime was my only crime. Still, like Cold Collation I could take it. I had letters to that effect from several serving women. The papers should hear of this.

# DAILY MIRROR

## Ace Filing Clerk To Be Axed Shock Horror etc.

> Today, Bombardier Milligan, the world-renowned corporal with three stripes, and known throughout the Italian theatre of war as the most advanced filing clerk in the British Army, heard that he was to be sacked.
>
> Reuter.

The band boys tried to commiserate with me. We had a last jam session in the band room and rounded off with a great piss up. I was carried to my room for the last time . . .

### A New Life and a New Dawn

A truck is waiting to take me away. How many times have I done this? Yet again the kit is piled in the back, and like a sheep to market, I am driven away, all on the whim of one man who thought I played my trumpet too loud. I am puzzling over what C P A means. Captain's Personal Assistant? Cracked People's Area? Clever Privates' Annexe? None of these, says the driver. It's 'Centril Pule of Hartists (Central Pool of Artists), hits a place where orl dhan-graded squaddies who can hentertain are sent.' Was he a down-graded entertainer?

'Yer.'

'What do you do?'

'Hi sing Hopera.'

'Opera?'

'Yer, you know, *La Bhome*, *Traviahta*, and the like.'

'Were you trained?'

'Now, it cum natural like.'

'Have you ever sung in opera natural like?'

'No, I just done the horditions like. The Captain says 'ees waitin' for a suitable vehicle for me.' Like a bus, I thought.

We have driven through Naples, turned left at the bottom of Via Roma up the Corso San Antonio, which goes on for ever in an Eastern direction. Finally we arrive at a broken-down Army Barracks complex. The walls are peeling, they look as if they have mange. I report to a Captain Philip Ridgeway, a sallow saturnine fellow with a Ronald Colman moustache who looks as if he has mange as well. He sits behind the desk with his hat on. He is the son of the famous Ridgeways' Late Joys Revue that led to the Players Theatre. He looks at my papers. 'So, you play the trumpet. Do you play it well?'

'Well, er loudly.'

'Do you read music?'

'Yes, and the *Daily Herald*.'

He smiled. He would find me a place in 'one of our orchestras'. I was taken by a Corporal Gron, who looked like an unflushed lavatory, and shown to a billet on the first floor, a room with forty single beds around the walls. In them were forty single men. This being Sunday, they were of a religious order that kept them in kip until midday. I drop my kit on a vacant bed, and it collapses to the floor. 'That's why it's vacant,' laughed Corporal Gron, who laughed when babies fell under buses. Next bed is Private Graham Barlow. He helps me repair the bed with some string and money. Nice man – he played the accordion. Noël Coward said, 'No gentleman would ever play the accordion.'

I had no job as such, and as such I had no job. Breakfast was at 8.30, no parade, hang around, lunch, hang further around, tea, extended hanging around, dinner and bed. The CPA Complex had the same ground plan as the Palace of Minos at Knossos, consisting of rehearsal rooms, music stores, costume stores, scenery dock and painting area, Wardrobe Mistress, Executive offices. People went in and were never seen again. The company was assembled from soldier artistes who had been down-graded. They would be formed into concert parties and sent on tour to entertain those Tommies who weren't down-graded. The blind leading the blind. The facilities were primitive, the lavatories were a line of holes in the ground. When I saw eighteen soldiers squatting/balancing over black holes with straining sweating faces for the first time, they looked like the start of the hundred yards for paraplegic dwarfs.

My first step to 'fame' came when I borrowed a guitar from the stores. I was playing in the rehearsal room when a tall cadaverous gunner said, 'You play the guitar then?' This was Bill Hall. If you've ever seen a picture of Niccolò Paganini, this was his double. What's more, he played the violin and played it superbly; be it a Max Bruch Concerto or I've Got Rhythm, he was a virtuoso. But bloody scruffy. We teamed up just for the fun of it, and in turn we were joined by Johnny Mulgrew, a short Scots lad from the Recce Corps; as he'd left them they were even shorter of Scots. Curriculum Vitae: Pre-war he played for Ambrose and the Inland Revenue. In the 56 Recce in N. Africa. Trapped behind enemy lines at Madjez-el-Bab. Lay doggo for forty-eight hours in freezing weather. Got pneumonia. Down-graded to B2 . . .

Together we sounded like Le Hot Club de France. When we played, other musicians would come and listen to us – a compliment – and it wasn't long before we were lined up for a show.

In the filling-in time, I used to play the trumpet in a scratch combination. It led to my meeting with someone from Mars, Gunner Secombe, H., singer and lunatic, a little myopic blubber of fat from Wales who had been pronounced a loony after a direct hit by an 88-mm gun in North Africa. He was asleep at the time and didn't know about it till he woke up. General Montgomery saw him and nearly surrendered. He spoke like a speeded up record, no one understood him, he didn't even understand himself; in fact, forty years later he was knighted for not being understood.

The Officers' Club, Naples. We were playing for dancing and cabaret, the latter being the lunatic Secombe. His 'music' consisted of some tatty bits of paper, two parts, one for the drums and one for the piano – the rest of us had to guess. We busked him on with 'I'm just wild about Harry'. He told us he had chosen it because his name was Harry, and we said how clever he was. He rushed on, chattering, screaming, farting, sweat pouring off him like a monsoon, and officers moved their chairs back. Then the thing started to shave itself, screaming, chattering and farting; he spoke at high speed; the audience thought he was an imported Polish comic, and many wished he was back in Warsaw being bombed. Shaving soap and hairs flew in all directions, then he launched into a screaming duet with himself, Nelson Eddie and Jeanette Macdonald, but you couldn't tell him apart. A few cries of 'hey hup' and a few more soapy farts, and he's gone, leaving the dance floor smothered in shaving soap. His wasn't an act, it was an interruption.

The dance continues, and officers are going arse over tip in dozens. 'No, not him,' they'd say when Secombe's name came up for a cabaret.

*Secombe, December 1945 – having cleared the Officers' Club, Naples, with screaming, raspberries, shaving and singing – well pleased*

Bill Hall. A law unto himself. He ignored all Army discipline, he ignored all civilian discipline. His regiment had despaired of him and posted him to CPA with an apology note.

Take kit parade. We are all at our beds, kit immaculately laid out for inspection. The Orderly Officer reaches Gunner Hall. There, on an ill-made bed, where there should be 19 items of army apparel, are a pair of socks, three jack-knives, a vest, a mess tin and a fork. The officer looks at the layout. He puts his glasses on.

OFFICER:          Where is the rest of your kit?
GUNNER HALL:   It's on holiday, sir.

Apart from Gunner Secombe, CPA contained other stars to be, including Norman Vaughan, Ken Platt and Les Henry, (who later formed The Three Monarchs).

*The CPA Personnel, including Spike Milligan (No. 1) and Harry Secombe (No. 2)*

There were, of course, failures. Private Dick Scratcher, down-graded with flat feet, was billed as The Great Zoll, the Voltage King. He was given a try-out at the now recovering Officers' Club. His act consisted of a 'Death Throne' made out of wood, cardboard and silver paper, with a surround of light bulbs. On a sign above was a warning: DANGER 1,000,000 VOLTS. The Great Zoll entered as a 'Sultan', with a turban that looked more like a badly bandaged head, and struck a 'gong' which was a dustbin lid painted with cheap silver paint: with its edge cut off it gave a flat 'CLANK'. He was assisted by the driver/opera singer clad in a loin cloth, his body stained brown with boot polish. The 'Sultan' would be strapped into the chair with silver straps, telling us all the while in Chinese with a north-country accent: 'Chop, chop, my assistant, Tong Bing, now strap me in Death t'chair, and throw switch, and send million volts through my t'body.' Tong Bing then chants some mindless tune which has nothing to do with the tune we are playing. Various bulbs go on and off as the great switch is thrown, the voltage meter goes up and down, the Great Zoll speaks: 'By power of t'mind I will resist the power of t'electricity.' He stares into space, then magnesium flashes go off and fill the club with choking smoke. The final magnesium flash has been placed too near The Great Zoll, it sets fire to his trousers. Tong Bing is trying to beat it out and the room is filled with watery-eyed coughing officers trying to escape.

Dick Scratcher's name went down next to Secombe's in the 'never again' list. After the war, Harry was appearing at the Palladium and was visited by the Great Zoll and his wife. Harry noticed that the woman's legs and arms were bandaged. 'I've changed the act,' says the Great Zoll. 'I'm into knife throwing.'

The best pianist in the CPA was Johnny Bornheim. Late nights we would play in the rehearsal room with a bottle of wine as company. Bornheim was a furrier in civvy street, but should have been a concert pianist. Self-taught, he could literally play anything.

He was fascinated with Bill Hall. He once pointed out, 'No one has ever seen Bill Hall's body alive!' True, he only showered after dark and likewise never took his clothes off with the light on. Was he hiding something? We decided to raid Bill Hall's body.

In darkness we wait by his bed. Comes 0200 hours, Bill shuffles in, he is undressing, he is down to his shirt and socks. Before he can enter his pit, we signal the lights on, and six of us seize him, remove his remaining garments, and hold him down, naked, struggling and swearing. I hold a clipboard with an anatomical list. Bornheim goes to work with a stick. He starts at the top.

'Head, one, with stray hairs attached plus dandruff.'

'Check.'

'Earoles and wax, two.'

'Check.'

'Neck, scrawny with Adam's apple, one.'

'Check.'

'Chest, sunken with stray hairs, one.'

'Check.'

'You bastards,' he is yelling and struggling.

'Legs, thin with lumps on knees, two.'

'Check.'

Bornheim elevates Hall's scrotum on the stick. 'Cobblers, red with purple tinges, two.'

'Check.'

'Chopper with foreskin attached, one.'

'Check.'

We released him and he chased us, hurling his and other people's boots. A drunken Secombe enters, sees the naked wraith, embraces him. 'My, you're looking lovely in the moonlight, Amanda.' Amanda says Piss Off. Hall has to fight off the insane raspberrying Welshman. If only his Queen could have seen him that night.

As to Trooper Johnny Mulgrew of Glasgow, he had a wicked sense of humour; his idea of a joke was a huge beaming woman in a wheelchair being pushed through Hyde Park by a dying cripple. Always good for a laugh.

## 'Over the Page'

This was the show that launched the Bill Hall Trio. It was the brainchild of Captain Hector Ross, whose play *Men in Shadow* I had destroyed at Maddaloni. It was sheer luck: one of the acts for *Over the Page* had withdrawn at the last moment, a sort of theatrical Coitus Interruptus. Could the Trio fill in? Yes. I knew that just playing jazz never was a winner, so I persuaded the wardrobe to give us the worst ragged costumes we could find. I worked out some patter and introductions. I never dreamed we would be anything more than just 'another act'. The set for *Over the Page* was a huge book.

Over the Page *stage set*

The artistes were a mixture of Italian professionals and soldier amateurs. Monday December 6th 1945 the show opened at the Bellini Theatre to a packed house. The write-up says it all:

Over the Page *orchestra*

*The male and female chorus from* Over the Page

*What the paper said: excerpt from the* Union Jack, December 12 1945

We were one incredible hit. When we came off, we were stunned. I couldn't believe that of all that talent out there, we had topped the lot. After the show, a Lieutenant Reg O'List of CPA came backstage. He had been a singer at the Windmill in London, which was rather like being a blood donor in a mortuary. He thinks we're great. Can he take us to dinner? God, we were in the big time already. Off the Via Roma is a wonderful pasta restaurant, we'll love it. Great! Lieutenant O'List does it in style, we go in a horse-drawn carriage. Bill Hall plays his violin as we drift down the Via Roma. Wow! Life is good. The restaurant is all one can dream of: the waiters wear white aprons, the tables have red and white check cloths, there's an oil lamp on every table, a mandolin band playing. As soon as we enter the waiters sweep us up in a cushion of hospitality. 'Si accomodo, accomodo,' a bottle of wine with the manager's compliments, thank you very much with our compliments. Giddy with success and a free dinner, we eat a mountain of spaghetti. Reg O'List can't stop telling us how good we are and we can't stop agreeing with him. He can't believe we are just the result of a chance meeting in a barrack room. Can we play some jazz after dinner? Yes. 'Hey! I know! why don't we

*The show-stopping Bill Hall Trio: J. Mulgrew on bass, Bill Hall on violin and Spike Milligan on guitar*

*Capt. Reg O'List, Pioneer Corps, playing and singing 'When they Begin the Beguine', Italy 1945*

put on a show?' etc! The customers stop eating, they cheer and clap, encore, encore. Free wine is slopping out of us. Enough is enough. Reg O'List is now very pissed; he will do *his* Windmill Act; he starts to sing 'Begin the Beguine'; he has a powerful shivery square voice.

'If he's from the Windmill,' says Gunner Hall, 'why doesn't he take his clothes off?' The night ends with Bill Hall splitting away from us – the last sight we had of him was on a tram playing opera to adoring passengers. What a night. It would lead us slowly down the road to oblivion.

# ROME AGAIN

# Rome Again

I'm going to Rome *again*! This time with a difference. No more three-ton trucks, but a charabanc! Our touring officer is Lieutenant Ronnie Priest, a misnomer if ever there was one. Ronnie looked like someone whose cab was off the road for repairs. His cockney accent clashes with the officer's uniform, but he does the job. The charabanc! stops at the hotel in Vuomero to pick up our Italian artistes. As the girls enter there's the usual 'Hello little darlin'' from the lads. Mitzi, the violin-accordion player, is Hungarian and forty-three; she's i/c the girl musicians and getting it from Franco Lati, our Charles Boyerish conductor (*see photo*). The route you all know by now. We arrive in Rome, Sunday evening, at the Albergo Universo. Spring beds! Sheets! En suite bathrooms!

Secombe and I share a room. Disaster. I am neat and tidy. Secombe is not. He hits the room like an exploding shell. One drawer a vest and a comb, a shoe wrapped up in an Army shirt, a broken bottle of Brylcreem wrapped in newspaper, a shaving brush with three hairs in a box, a towel shot with holes, mess tins stuck with toothpaste. If a Red Cross official had been present he would have been declared a disaster area. Secombe was a mass of nervous energy, he went in all directions at once – you needed a man-size flyswat to catch him. Whichever part of the room you went, he was there first; if you looked in a mirror, he was looking back at you. He gave off long bursts of garbled conversation, interspersed with raspberries and bits of songs. His record for staying in one place was three seconds. Having spread his kit like a plague around the room he was massaging his head with Brylcreem, and singing, raspberrying, insane laughter, and babbling: 'Rome, Rome ha ha ha, lovely Rome, ha ha ha raspberry . . . Pretty girls pretty girls . . . ha ha ha, scream, raspberry' and was gone. I dined alone in the hotel. The manageress: 'Was everything alright, signor?' No, could she kill Secombe? She is a strapping thirty-year-old with black Eton-cropped hair; she joins me for coffee. She had been an Olympic athlete, a javelin thrower.

Would I like to have tea with her some time and see her javelino? Yes. I retire to my wonderful room, I luxuriate in the bath and watch the bubbles rise. Wearing my now splodgy blue pyjamas I slide slowly between the sheets. Ahhh!

> Oh wonderful clean sheets
> One of nature's real treats
> Tho' my pyjamas don't look very good
> It's better than walking the streets.
>                     W. McGonagall

Around about midnight I have written several letters and am reading an anthology of British Verse printed in Italy. I'm skimming through Shakespeare's Sonnets and in comes Staggering L/Bdr Secombe, ha ha, he has that huge grin with revolving teeth. 'Hello, hello, hoo! up! scream! raspberry: Whoops.' He gets up again. 'Spike, do you like beer?' Yes, he empties a bottle of it over me, screams with laughter, falls back on the bed, which collapses, and goes into a deep cross-eyed grinning sleep. Thank God, he's unconscious. I strip off my sodden pyjamas, take a shower, and when I get back he's gone!!! No, no, he's hammering on the door, he thought he was going into the bathroom and went into the hall. I let the chattering farting thing in, he lets go with a few top C's and vanishes into the bathroom. There's a great crash as he does something or other. I put my beer-soaked pillows on his bed and take his.

He didn't come out of the bathroom. Next morning I found him asleep in his bath, an idiotic smile on his face and one boot off. God, Wales has a lot to answer for.

He arises and is full of the joys of chattering, farting, singing and cries of Hey hup la! He's down the stairs like a clockwork doll, into the dining-room, eats six breakfasts, sings, whistles and farts his way through ten cups of tea. Where was he last night? He went to a dance, met a pretty signorina hoi hup! and in a moment of Welsh hieraith hoi! hup! gave her his leather Army jerkin. From now on he *froze*.

# PALESTINE

## CPA show is a fine effort

### By ANDY GRAY

ARMY Welfare's Central Pool of Artists is to be congratulated on producing a first class, ambitious show in "Over the Page" at the Argentina Theatre, Rome, this week. The production is to tour Italy.

Probably on as large a scale as anything Ensa has presented from England, the attractive main set and sub-sets, the many colourful costumes, the abundant talent is all "made in Italy" by the C.P.A. The production, overlooking first night worries, is unusually slick, carefully planned and luxuriously carried out, a fitting climax to Capt. Hector Ross's long and ever-progressive career as O.C., Central Pool of Artists.

A special hand to Luisa Poselli. She'll be the first to admit that her act was far from scratch on Monday, due to lack of co-operation and understanding between herself and her accompaniment, which at times faded to nothing, but she stuck it out and after a woeful Chattanooga Choo Choo, which she won't forget in a hurry, she won her way to the biggest applause of the night with her dancing feet. A smaller artist would have walked off—Luisa is a big artist.

Nimble Bob Wayne, with his hat and cane, got the show off to a good start, followed by Jean Weir and Mary Doolan dancing in various tempos. Harry Secombe's Col. Scratch was just right and the Lady of Fashion production number was as ambitious as I've seen overseas.

Bill Clafton, entertaining since North African days, excelled himself with his Egyptian dance.

Mary Doolan's noted Indian dance was above average and Flashback slickly done by Harry Secombe, Jan Acton, Bill Gill and Billy Howard.

Graham Barlow and Yutzi Kugli proved that accordions are still as popular as ever and then rubber-panned, burlesquing Harry Secombe proved that he has a big and bright future ahead of him in British music hall sketches when he gave us his A.T.S. officer, his voice-pill seller, his nervous man at a village concert and his western drummer in quick succession.

The hit of the night was Bill Hall's trio. Bill's eccentric hot fiddling will take him far and his partners on bass and guitar make up the best act of the night.

The show opened at the Argentina Theatre; again the Bill Hall Trio are the hit of the show.

The act was basically very fast jazz numbers; 'Honeysuckle Rose', then 'The Flight of the Bumble Bee', 'Tiger Rag', all with visual gags. The response was unbelievable; we realized that here we might have something that would have great potential in civvy street.

*The Alexander Club, Rome, Harry Secombe* (l) *willing Johnny Mulgrew* (r) *to pay the bill. Bob Wayne standing.*

Life was really better than I had ever had it. First-class hotel accommodation, food, free all day, and a roaring success at night. Tomorrow didn't matter, except it kept arriving. By day we'd swan around Rome with the inevitable visit to the Alexander Club.

We had a sword of Damocles. It was Bill Hall. He was itinerant, and we never knew where he was or what he was doing. After the show he'd disappear into the Rome night and its naughty areas and we wouldn't see him till a few minutes before we were due back on stage. It got so bad that I would go on stage without him even being in the theatre; it was then I started to tell jokes just to hold the fort.

*Spike on top of the Colosseum*

# BOLOGNA

## Bologna

*Sunday*. We are off to Bologna. Where the hell is Bill Hall?
Someone says Italy! We search the hotel, then his room;
there's nothing in it though he's slept in both beds, left a tap
running, and a pair of socks in the sink. Wait, what is this
unshaven wreck with a violin case? It is he. He gets on the
charabanc, ignoring the fact that we've been waiting half an
hour. A desultory cheer greets him. Totally unmoved, he sits
down. I watch a drip from his nose fall and extinguish his
dog-end. I am seated at the back on a bench seat. I have
placed my guitar case on the luggage rack and as we start, it
falls off on to Hall's head. 'You have-a musica on yewer
brayne,' says Mitzi. It is a good joke for a forty-three-year-
old Hungarian accordion player.

We are heading inland and it's snowing. NO car heaters
in those days! We are climbing the narrow road up the
Apennines, and it's getting colder. All is not well. Nino the
driver is shouting and praying in a stricken voice, the roads
are very slippery, we'll have to put the skid chains on. We set
to, straining and swearing. 'What a bleedin' liberty,' says
Gunner Hall. 'How can you put bloody skid chains on and
be expected to play the violin.' Lieutenant Priest answers
that there's no need to play the violin when putting the skid
chains on but as Gunner Hall is just standing and watching,
it would help if he did. Fingers are aching with cold; finally
it's done; a quick drink of hot tea from the thermos and
we're off again. We are at three thousand feet, heavy snow,
icy roads, very dark and very cold. We have all gone quiet as
we sense that the driver Nino is none too brave. Then the
sound of Hall's violin playing 'I'm Dreaming of a White
Christmas'. There's a lot of laughter, then we all join in.
Varied lyrics: 'I'm dreaming of a white mistress', or 'I'm
steaming on an old mattress'. Quiet again. We pass a chiesa,
it's ringing out the Angelus; several of the Italian girls cross
themselves.

'I don't understand 'em,' says Bill Hall. 'Last night they
were all screwing themselves silly.'

Lieutenant Priest passes sandwiches down the charabanc. 'Ham and cheese,' he says. We are all stamping our feet and blowing into cupped hands. Sometimes we cupped our feet and stamped our hands: variety is the spice of life. It was an awful long cold boring darkness. It wasn't a moment too soon when we arrived in Bologna; with the Tower of Dante looming into the night sky, we pull up at the Albergo Oralogio. A fin de cycle building. All is Baroque, even the porters.

We are soon in wonderful bedrooms, faded but lovely. I have a huge marble bath with gorgon-headed taps, and a giant brass shower rose in a wooden boxed-in cabinet. The curtains are damask. It's a single room, so I'm safe from singing, farting, chattering Secombe.

'Hey, come and ha' a drink, Spike.' It's Mulgrew, he's found a vino bar right next door. 'We could do with one after that bloody journey.' OK. I join him. The manageress falls for Johnny.

*Mulgrew set fair for free drinks*

The vino bar is the meeting place of all the local footballers. They have money, do we have anything to sell. Mulgrew puts up his soul. I have a fine officer's raincoat given me by my father. Can they see it? Not from here. I dash into the Albergo and return gasping. Oh, I'm in no hurry to sell, you understand, but how much? Five thousand lire. The word thousand disorientates the mind. Used to humble one, two, three in sterling but five thousand! Rich! rich! rich! Wrong! wrong! wrong! little international banker. It came to four quid: and it cost fifteen! It was brand new, and there it is going out the door to a football match. Still, four quid was four quid, but it wasn't fifteen.

Tired by the trip, elated by the five thousand lire, pissed by the wine, I retired to my Baroque bedroom, laid out my mottled blue pyjamas, took a marble bath, a brass shower, got into the Baroque bed and rang for room service. There's bugger all: room service is 'finito'. What have they got? La fredda colazione!! Argggh, well it was better than nothing, though when it arrived I realized it wasn't. What's the old waiter hanging about for? All service after ten has to be paid for by cash. What? But I'm travelling on the King's warrant, this trip is all found. Well find a tip. No! OK, he'll call the manager. No, no, OK, I pay. Has he got change for a ten thousand lire note? Yes, he says, have I been selling raincoats to those footballers?

Again the Bill Hall Triumph. It's getting to be a habit. With the raincoat money I brought an old Kodak camera. I filmed everything, see over:

The streets of Bologna were swarming with Italian Partisans wearing bandoliers, their belts stuffed with German stick grenades. They sauntered the sidewalks with a braggadocio air, waving their captured weapons and shouting Viva Italia. After a while it got a bit boring and Bill Hall said to one, 'Le Guerre Finito mate.' We climbed the six hundred steps up the Tower of Dante, only to find graffiti: 'Viva La Figa.'

*Spike feeding the pigeons in a piazza in Bologna. Photograph of no particular merit other than that the photographer would one day arise and find Sir in front of his name.*

## Christmas in Italy

Our last show in Bologna was on Christmas Day. It was all very strange. On Christmas Eve, after a show to a very inebriated audience, I wanted to be alone. I went to my bedroom and wished I could be back at 50 Riseldine Road with my mum and dad and brother. I wanted that little Christmas tree in the front room, the coal fire especially lit to 'air the room' for Christmas Day. The simple presents, a scarf, a pair of socks, a presentation box of 25 Player's cigarettes, my brother's box of Brittans soldiers, a drawing book with a set of pencils. Very modest fare by modern standards, but to me then, still simple and unsophisticated, it was a warming and magic day. The lunch, and *chicken*, that was something! In 1939, chicken was a luxury. And the tin of Danish ham! The huge trifle with custard and real CREAM. My father's pride in opening the Port, pretending he was a savant, smelling the cork. 'Ahhhh yes,' he would say, and pour it with the gesture of a sommelier at the Lord Mayor's banquet.

Here I was in a room in Bologna. I couldn't get it together. Outside there is roistering. Not me. I knew tomorrow there would be no stocking at the end of my bed. Father Christmas was a casualty of World War Two.

# FLORENCE

## Florence

City of Medicis, Savonarola, and chattering raspberrying
Secombe, now freezing without his leather 'love gift' jerkin.
This is the city of the artist, the artisan, the connoisseur.
Our Hotel Dante is just round the corner from the Piazza del
Signoria. I would be able to see places that I had only read
about. The hotel is one built for those rich Victorians doing
the Grand Tour. Sumptuous rooms, a wonderful double bed
with duck eider, like sleeping in froth. Putting my egg-stained
battledress in the bevelled glass and walnut cupboard was like
wearing a flat hat in the Ritz. Secombe flies past chattering
and farting up the Carrara marble stairs with its flanking
Venetian balustrades topped with cherubim holding bronze
lanterns. He looks totally out of place, he belongs at the pit
head.

I am standing on the spot, explaining that this is where
Savonarola was burned. 'Oo was Savonarola?' says Gunner
Hall. I tell him 'oo he is'. 'They *burnt* him?' Yes. 'Why. Were
they short of coal?' I explain that he was at odds with the
Medici and the state of Florence. 'Fancy,' says Hall. 'Why
didn't 'e call the fire brigade?' The same indifference applies
to see Cellini's Perseus. With the head of Medusa, Hall wants
to know why statues are erected to people being burnt or
having their heads chopped off. 'Why not someone normal
like Tommy Handley?' Yes, of course: 'Here is Cellini's statue
of Tommy Handley from I T M A.' That would look really
nice in the Piazza.

The Pitti Palace leaves me stunned; masterpiece after
masterpiece, there's no end to it. From Titian to Seguantini.
You come out feeling useless and ugly. On the Ponte Vecchio
Secombe and I ask Hall to take a photo of us. It comes out
with the wall behind us in perfect focus, two blurred faces in
the foreground. He was well pleased.

Now a divertimento. An English lady living in Florence
has invited us to tea. She is Madame Penelope Morris, a
'relative' of William Morris, 'the man who invented wallpaper'. She was sixty-nine, tall, thin, a white translucent

skin with the veins visible; her neck looked like a map of the
Dutch canal system. She wore swathes of bead necklaces – to
the value of two shillings. Two pale blue eyes, very close
together, sat atop a long bulbous nose. She had no waist, no
bottom or bosom; she went straight up and down like a
phone box. A small crimped rouged mouth like a chicken's
bum. She spoke with an upper-class adenoidal voice that put
her next in line to the throne. She ushered us into a cloying
room that smelt of stale unemptied sherry glasses and tom-
cat piss. We sat in well-worn chairs with antimacassars. She
rang a brass bell, the clanger fell out. 'It's always doing
that.' The summons brought a thousand-year-old butler
carrying a papier-mâché tray loaded with what looked like
papier-mâché cakes. The tea ritual. 'The cakes are made
locally,' she said, and should have added 'by stonemasons.'
It was all a ploy. She is a spiritualist in need. So, would we
boys like a séance? So saying she pulls the curtains and we sit
at a circular table not knowing what to expect. Now, would
anyone like to get in touch with a loved one? Yes, says
Marine Paul Robson, one of our shanghaied dancers. 'I'd
like to get in touch with my mother Rosie.' Mrs Morris goes
into a trance. 'Are you there Mrs Robson, are you there
Rosie . . .' A little louder. 'Are you there Mrs Rosie Robson
. . .' She opens her eyes. 'She's not hearing me.' What Robson
hadn't told her was that his mother wasn't dead, but was
living in Brighton. 'She won't be able to hear from here,' he
said to a slightly bemused Mrs Morris.

Does anyone else want to get in touch? Yes. Bill Hall
would like to contact his grandmother Lucy. Forewarned,
Mrs Morris asks, 'Is she dead?'

'I hope so,' says Hall. 'They buried her.'

'Are you there, Mrs Lucy Hall?' she intones, eyelids flutter-
ing, as she places a collection box on the table, giving it a
shake to agitate the coins inside. Suddenly Paul Robson lets
out a scream and runs from the room. Mrs Morris calls a halt;
he has ruined the 'balance'. We must all leave now as she is
expecting another 'tea party'. In the hall we meet a group of

unsuspecting soldiers who can't understand our stifled laughter.

We ask Robson why he had run out screaming. He says, 'I felt there was something nasty in the room.'

'There was,' says Bill Hall. 'The cat done it.'

Secombe and I have hit it off with two waitresses at the hotel. One fat, one thin. He calls them Laurel and Hardy. They weren't exactly beauties, but then neither was Secombe or I.

*Hardy (mine) 12 stone 3 lb*          *Laurel (Secombe's) 7 stone 3 lb*

We would meet them 'dopo lavoro'. They will show us a 'nice Boogie Woogie Club'. It sounded like a weapon. By the

231

kitchen we waited, our romantic interlude broken only by the slops boy emptying rubbish into the reeking bins. Finally they appear, smelling of cheap perfume and washing up water. Secombe give me Hardy. She's too full for him. We were taken to what by day was a sewer. An Italian trio are trying to catch up with the jazz scene. Through a fug, a blue-chinned waiter shows us to a table the size of a playing card. By intertwining knees we are seated, we appear glued together. Secombe is chattering in Anglo-Italian: 'You molto bello,' he tells Laurel. There's another fine mess he's got us into. We drink some appalling cheap red wine that leaves a purple ring round the mouth; Secombe looks like a vampire. Laurel takes Secombe to do the 'Jitterbuggery' and they are lost in the steaming mêlée. I too am sucked in by Hardy. I am trying to move her bulk round the floor, but I really need a heavy goods licence. Still, it was nice holding a girl, even if her load had shifted. A gyrating, arm-pumping, steaming, farting and chattering, all teeth and glasses Secombe zooms past. 'Having fun?' he shouts. So that's what it is. Away he goes in twenty different directions. It's getting on for two a.m. The girls say they must 'andare a casa', they have work in the morning. There follows the traditional groping and steaming in the doorway. A mist has risen from the Arno, infiltrating the town and Secombe's trousers. I can hear the hiss of steam as cold air hits his boiling body. We depart virgo intacto, trousers bursting with revolving testicles and dying erections. We retrace our steps to the hotel. We are lost. 'Fancy,' says Secombe. 'Who in the Mumbles would dream that I was lost in Florence?' I tell him I gave up: who in Mumbles would know he was lost in Florence.

A tart hovers by. Lily Marlene? She knows the way to the hotel. Do we want a shag? It's only fifty lire after ten, she'll do us both for forty. Sorry dear, we're training for the priesthood. OK, we can find our own fucking way back. Finally we did. 'Home at last,' says Secombe, 'and forty lire to the good.'

No, not home at last, locked out at last. 'Open up landlord, we are thirsty travellers.' We rang the bell. We hammered on the door. We tapped on the windows. We shouted upwards. We hammered on the bell. We rang the door. We tapped upwards. We shouted on the windows. 'How much did she say for the two of us?' says Secombe. A sliding of bolts, a weary concierge opens the door. 'Molto tardi signorini,' he says. We apologize. I press a ten lire note in his hand. A low moan comes from his lips. 'What did you give him?' says Secombe. 'A heart attack.'

I crawl into my dream bed. Peace. Relaxation, but no, wait!!! Something wet and 'horribule' is in my bed. It's a terrible soldier joke, there in my bed is an eight-inch 'Richard the Third', made from dampened brown paper. Wait, there's a note, a chilling message. It says: 'The phantom strikes again.' It bears all the hallmarks of Mulgrew, or is it the Mulgrew marks of Hall? I fell asleep laughing.

# RETURN TO NAPLES

## Return to Naples

Days seem to go by like water rushing over stones. We leave Florence, having visited every possible sight. It was a city I can never forget. We are to return to Naples, with an overnight stay in Rome. There we dine again with the Eton-cropped manageress, whom we now know to be a lesbian. The discovery was made by Lt. Priest who had put his hand on her leg and had it crushed in a vice-like grip, all the while smiling sweetly at him. I got a bit worried when she said to me, 'You are a very pretty boy.' After dinner she asked the trio to come to her room and play. Drinks had been laid on, including a Barolo 1930! She asked us to play 'You Go to my Head', then sang it in Italian in a deep baritone voice. If we weren't certain before, we were now. Yes, there was the shaving soap on the windowsill. The more she drank, the more masculine she became, giving us thumps on the back like demolition hammers. 'Let's get out of here,' said Hall, 'or she'll fuck the lot of us.'

The last leg to Naples. All the while Secombe entertains us with insane jokes and raspberries. Does anyone know the Big Horse Song? No. He sings Big Horse I love you. The Hook and Eye song? No? He sings Hook and I live without you. The Niton Song? Niton day, you are the One. The Ammonia song? Ammonia bird in a gilded cage. There was no stopping him, he was like a dynamo.

'Are you on anything!' I said.

'Yes, two pound ten a week. Hoi Hup, raspberry.' He used to be a pithead clerk.

'Were you good at figures?'

'Well, as long as I got within three or four shillings.'

If what he told me was true, miners who hadn't shown up for a week ended up with double wages and the reverse. The day he joined the army, the miners held a pithead Thanksgiving Service.

Back in the old routine. Hall has been missing for days. During his absence, we transform his army bed into a

237

magnificent four poster with a Heraldic Shield, satin drapes and a scarlet velvet bedspread. We time it to perfection. Hall comes in five minutes before the once-weekly roll call and inspection. He walks in a moment before the Inspecting Officer. Stunned, he stands by his bed. Enter Captain O'List. He too is stunned.

O'LIST:    Whose bed is this?
HALL:      Mine sir.
O'LIST:    How long has it been like this?
HALL:      Just today, sir.
O'LIST:    Why?
HALL:      It's my mother's birthday, sir.

O'List couldn't contain himself. Weak-legged he walked rapidly from the room. On the stairs we could hear him choking with laughter.

# BARI

# Bari

Yes, we are to ancient Barium where the meal-enema was invented. We are to entertain the bored soldiery. First thing, chain Gunner Hall to the bed. Louisa Pucelli, our Italian star, has dropped out of the show, and in her place we have Signorina Delores Bagitta, an ageing bottle-blonde Neapolitan old boiler, with a voice like a Ferrari exhaust. She looked O K from a distance, about a mile I'd say. She did a Carmen Miranda act, her layers of cutaneous fat shuddering with every move. 'Amore, amore,' she'd croak. It was monumental tat.

Bari is a dusty seaport on the Adriatic. There's Bari Vecchio and Bari Nuovo. No hotel this time, but a large hostel that seemed to be under permanent siege by lady cleaners. Even as you sat on the W C a mop would suddenly slosh under the door. The streets are heavy with bored British troops, and a heavy sprinkling of Scots from the tribal areas. The old city is really a museum piece, it's a time capsule dated about 1700: the Moors were here and left their mark — many a dark skin can be seen.

Secombe appears to be inflating his head; he is even inflating his face. Somehow the wind is escaping upwards. No, the man is in real trouble. Poor Gunner, struck down in his prime! Of all things he has illness of the face. It's true, folks, he has been using cheap Italian make-up which has affected all the cuts he gave himself during his screaming farting and shaving act. It gets bad, and the swelling closes both eyes. There was little pity. We had warned him if he didn't stop it, this is what would happen. The dramatic situation of temporary blindness gives Secombe a great chance for histrionics: he becomes Gunner King Lear. 'I'm sorry lads, to have let you down like this, but remember the show must go on.' He lay in his bed, not knowing that we had left the room. He develops a high temperature which speeds him up. When the ambulance arrives to take him, he is chattering, screaming and farting at twice the speed. 'I'm sorry I'm leaving you lads, but I'll be back, the show must go on, thanks for all your help, remember me when you're on stage, tell the lads I did my best, Cardiff 3 Swansea Nil. Lloyd George knew my father, saucepanbach, Ivor Novello, when I come home again to Wales.' As they drove him away we could hear snatches of Welsh songs, rugby scores, raspberrying and screaming. When he arrived at Bari General Hospital they took him straight to the psychiatric ward where he gave three doctors a nervous breakdown.

His place in the show was taken by Delores Bagitta; dressed as a nun she sang 'Ave Maria' in a gin-soaked voice. Lt. Priest pleaded with her not to, but to our horror and amazement she got an ovation! There's no telling.

Surprise, surprise, after our first show, who shows up? It's lean lovely Lance-Bombardier Reg Bennett. What's he doing here? He was posted. He arrived with a letter to the Town Major who said. 'I see Bennett that you are an expert on heavy dock clearance and port maintenance.'

'No sir, I'm an insurance clerk.'

Someone had blundered. He gets the plum job of Town Major's clerk. With it goes a private flat above his office. He invited me back. We took a taxi, so he was doing alright. We arrived at the flat and opened the door to find the Town Major screwing some Iti bird on the floor. 'I'm afraid the room is occupied,' he said.

We ended up at a restaurant in the Old Town; customers are up-market Italians and a few British officers. 'All black market,' says Reg.

'How can you afford all this, Reg?'

He grinned the grin of a man heavily involved in skullduggery. 'I handle the NAAFI,' he said. Ah! NAAFI, the crown jewels of military life. We spoke about an idea we had had back in Baiano. A nightclub on the Thames. It was pie in the sky. Bennett says. 'Milligan, if we're going to dream, why stop at a night club on the Thames, why not a hundred-storey hotel in San Francisco? We've just had four bloody years of war, why go in for more trouble? No Spike, I've thought about it, if we all clubbed together we'd just about afford two tables and six chairs.'

'We could get a bank loan.'

'OK, *eight* chairs then.'

He was right. I said so: 'You are right.' I said, 'To hell with the hundred-storey hotel and the six chairs. Waiter, another bottle of Orvieto!'

Well pissed, Bennett dropped me off at the hotel. An hour later he appears at my bedroom door. 'He's still screwing,' he said. I put him in the spare bed. 'I'm not angry, just jealous,' he said. Reg departed next morning. I was not to see him for another five years, by which time the Town Major had finished screwing.

The sound of chattering, farting and screams tells me that Secombe has been cured and released, and the hospital burnt down for safety. 'Hello hello, hey hoi hup, raspberry, scream, sing, on with the show hey hoi hup.' He revolves round the hotel at speed. What had eluded scientists for 2000 years has been discovered by Gunner Secombe. Perpetual motion.

## New Year's Eve

A.D. 1946 is a few hours away as the show opens. The front row is filled with the well-scrubbed, pink and pretty Queen Alexandra Nursing Sisters, all crisp and starched in their grey, white and red uniforms. Hovering above them in the crammed gallery are hundreds of steaming Highlanders, all in the combustible atmosphere of whisky fumes. The Bill Hall Trio are a smash hit. We are going for an encore when to our horror we see, falling like gentle rain from heaven, scores of inflated rubber condoms floating down on the dear nursing sisters. Some, all merry with the festive season, start bursting them before they scream with realization. Military police go in among the steaming Scots and a fight breaks out; to the sound of smashing bottles, thuds, screams, wallops and yells, a nun sings 'Ave Maria'. Happy New Year everyone.

After the show there's a party on stage, a table with ARGGGGHHH Cold Collation, the Bill Hall Trio play for dancing. A good time was had by all, and something else

243

had by all was Delores Bagitta. Lt. Priest drinks a toast: 'This is our last show and we will be returning to base tomorrow.'

## Naples Again

It is 120 miles to Naples, a sort of London/Birmingham trip. Bill, Johnny and I sit as usual at the back on the bench seat. We start to talk seriously about a future in England. We agree to stick together and make our fortune. With the reception we've been getting, how can we go wrong.

## January. CPA Barracks

It was a sybaritic life. No parades, an occasional inspection, and a NAAFI open day. There were perks. 'There's spare tickets for the opera,' says gay Captain Lees, who is ever so lonely and rightfully in the Queen's Regiment. The opera? Fat men and women bawling at each other in front of cardboard trees, backed by a crowd of hairy-legged spearmen. OK, it was free. I was about to see what any opera lover would give his life for. Outside the San Carlo: 'The WVS presents the world's greatest tenor, Benjamino Gigli.' Gigli? Coleman Hawkins or Ben Webster, yes, but Gigli?

I have a plush box to myself it seems, but just before curtain-up a smelly Italian peasant carrying a bag of food and a bottle of wine is ushered in. 'Scusi,' he says, then starts laying the food out on a cloth. Overture, curtain up. Magic. Where have I been? Puccini! What an ignorant bastard I've been. Wait, the Italian is getting pissed, and by the time Mimi's tiny hand is frozen, he's joining in the arias. He's sitting on the floor, the audience can't really see him, they're all shushing at *me*. The attendants come in, I have a struggle telling them I'm not the culprit. Eventually they drag the protesting Iti away, but leave his bread, cheese and wine which I am well pleased to finish.

The Opera continues. 'Mimi' sob, sob goes Rudolph, and

crashes his twenty stone on top of the poor consumptive; the curtain comes down to stop her being asphyxiated. Curtain call after curtain call. I am on my feet shouting Beeeeseeee! Like all bloody musicians, the orchestra are trying to get out before any encores ... they all escape but Gigli collars the harpist and sings Neapolitan folksongs, for an hour – magic. Gigli is gone to his rest, but that evening goes on ...

## A Bitter End

The curse of the working class! Piles! I am stricken, strucken and stracken with the things! Unlike other enemies, one could not come face to face with these things. Piles! The MO is no help: he is twiddling *his* things and unsympathetic.

'There's the operation,' he says.

'And it's agony,' says I.

'That is true,' says he. Otherwise ... what then? He shrugs his shoulders. I'm pretty sure that shrugging your shoulders is no cure for a sore arse. He gives me a pot of foul-smelling ointment. 'Apply to the parts.'

Parts? Piles don't have parts. I can have two days in bed and then come and see him again. The pretty Italian lady cleaners want to know why I'm in bed. No way will my romantic soul let me tell them it's piles, not even in Italian. Piles-o! No! I have bronchitis. They want to know why every time I sneeze, I grab my arse and scream. It's very difficult. The Duty Officer and Sergeant find me asleep face down-wards at midday.

'Why is this man in bed, Sergeant?'

'Piles, sir.'

'Piles?'

'Yes sir, the piles.'

'Have you seen the MO?'

'Yes, sir.'

'What's he say?'

'He said I had piles, bed down for two days.'

The Officer gave me a look of utter disdain. Why? He was

> **WHITEHALL. FIELD·MARSHALL ALEXANDER'S OFFICE**
>
> ALEXANDER stands in front of a huge war map. HIGH-RANKING OFFICERS WAIT ON HIS EVERY WORD, HE POINTS TO THE MAP.
>
> ALEXANDER: Gentlemen (*points to flags on map*), there are several outbreaks of pile jealousy in these areas.
>
> GENERALS: Scrampson – Scrampson – Scrampson!!!
>
> ALEXANDER: From now on, all cases of piles must be kept top secret.

*jealous.* Any man with such a demeaning illness as piles should never be allowed to shirk his duty. Officers never had piles and if they did they went on serving the King.

## Romance 'Neath Italian Skies

The music of 'Lae thar piss tub dawn bab' floats on the air. It's spring in Napoli! Bornheim and I are sipping sweet tea as the sun streams into the golden pilasters of the Banqueting Room of the Royal Palace, Naples NAAFI, having posted a look out on the roof for Gracie Fields. Our waitress is a Maria, and fancying me.

'Wot ewer name?'

'Spike.'

'Spak?'

'Yes, Spike.'

'Spak.'

It sounds like custard hitting a wall. My darling, can we go 'passagiere sul la Mare?' Si, si, si. When darling? Sabato. But we must be careful, we must not be seen by her parents or her familyo! Why, Maria, why? Wasn't it I, a British soldier, who has liberated Italy from the Naughty Nazis and let loose a hoard of raping, pillaging, Allied soldiers on to

*Maria in a state of High Anxiety at the start of our day out*

your streets. Does her family know I am a Holy Roman Catholic with half a hundredweight of relics of the cross to my credit, *and* a cache of secondhand underwear? No, no, no, it would be dangerous. What would happen if they caught us together? They would catch mine together and crush them. We meet then in the mysterious Vomero, she in Sunday best, me in the best I can find on Sunday. Now for a day of high romance. But no. She is in a state of high anxiety, every ten seconds she clutches me with a stifled scream, she imagines one of her family appearing, knife in hand. We spend the day like two people trying to avoid the searchlights at Alcatraz, forever flattening against walls, diving into dark doorways where I give them a quick squeeze, and running across squares.* At the end of the day, shagged out by a

* One of the squares I ran across was Reg O'List.

247

hard day's espionage and squeezing, she says goodbye and catches a tram. Bornheim is sitting on his bed awaiting the results.

'Did you get it?'

'No.'

Nothing? No. What did I do? About eighteen miles, I said.

# CAPRI

## 'Twas on the Isle of Capri

Private Bornheim is singing the theme from the 'Pathétique' and cutting his toe-nails with what look like garden shears. 'The good weather is coming, we should go for a trip to Capri.' Good idea, but we must choose a day when Gracie Fields is singing on the mainland. Ha ha ha. 'When should we go?' As soon as he's finished cutting his toe-nails. That could be weeks.

*The quay for the ferry to Capri – left is the Castel Uovo*

One fine warm spring morning, we board the ferry *Cavallo del Mare*, and set fair for the Isle of Capri. Bornheim feels fine: with toe-nails clipped he's about ten pounds lighter. A bar on board sells cigarettes, fruit juices and flies.

I watch as the magic isle heaves into view, blue and purple in the morning mist, the old village in the centre, the houses huddled together like frightened children. On the bridge an unshaven captain in a vest, oily peaked cap and flies, shouts

*Bornheim holding his eternal* Union Jack *newspaper – with a passing Maria*

to the shoreman. We approach Marina Grande, he cuts the engines, we glide to the quay; all the while Private Bornheim has been immersed in his Union Jack, calling out bits of news: 'They've increased the fat allowance back home.' All that and Capri!

As we disembark, Italian Dragomen and flies are waiting. 'Do you like a donkey?' No thanks, I'm a vegetarian. We board the Funicolare – up up up. At the top we walk out into the most famous square in the world, Captain Reg O'List. How are we? – he's just returning. Goodbye Reg, no – no need to sing 'Begin the Beguine', no, thank mother for the rabbit.

The main square is set up with cafés and outdoor tables, no piped music or transistors. We choose the Café Azzura because it's nearest, and order two icecreams. What icecreams!!! Wow, a foot high, multi-coloured, and covered in cream and flies. We are the only two soldiers in the Square.

My God! the impossible! ''Ello lads.' It's *her*! It's our Gracie! I wished it was *theirs*. She insists we come and have a 'nice cup of tea'. Down the lanes she takes us to her Villa

Canzone del t'mare; the view is stunning but the house is rather like a very good class boarding-house in Scunthorpe. She's wonderfully warm-hearted. We sit on the balcony admiring the view; please God, don't let her sing. Is she going to say it? She does. 'Ee Bai Gom, a bit different from Blackpool.' She *must* be working from a script. We escape without any singing. 'Good luck lads, give my love t'folks back t'ome.' We'd escaped! Not even 'Sally'!

I wanted to see San Michele. It's closed, says a caretaker who looked like Frankenstein's monster without the bolts. On to the site of the Villa of Tiberius, now carefully converted into cowsheds. Sloshing thru' cow dung, a local shows where Tiberius threw his victims over the cliff.

'I don't see what's dangerous about that,' said Bornheim. 'It's perfectly safe until you hit the rocks.'

Lunch, midday and that warm torpor was implemented as we ate Spaghetti Marinara and drank Ruffino at a little restaurant, high over the sea.

*Me after the meal, well fed and pissed. Observe geranium.*

As I write this nearly forty years later, I can still feel the warmth of that day; that one day can cast such a lasting spell speaks either for my appreciation of life, or that ancient Capri was indeed as charged with such beauty that it left itself tattooed on your mind, soul and spirit. I know I was quite a simple soldier, unsophisticated, but as I grew older, my mind took up the slack of that past time and computed it into a finely honed memory, leaving every colour, taste, sound and sight as crisp and as electric as though it happened yesterday; and to me as I write, it did.

I remember a potted geranium on the wall. I wonder if it remembers me. It's scarlet luminescence, projected against a fibrillating azure sea, seemed to hypnotize me. Like all idiots with a camera, I had to photograph it, and like all dodos who think they can capture their emotions on a holiday snap, I took a colour picture, in black and white . . .

*The world's first colour photograph in black and white*

I must be Irish. Well, I was that day.

'It's the colour of the sea,' said Bornheim, equally pissed.

'What about the colour?' I'm asking.

'It looks as if it's been painted,' he said, staring into its calling waters. 'It has been,' I said.

'*Who was he?*' said Bornheim, stressing every word. That geranium, it was becoming fluorescent: I think it was doing to me what the chair did to Aldous Huxley in *The Doors of Perception*. I was understanding why Van Gough painted that simple chair in Arles – people say he created his own mescalin. What a saving! I sat on the wall and looked towards the Capri headland and envisaged the marble palace of Tiberius that once adorned it. That a man so innately evil should have lived in such beauty; poor Mallonia killing herself ('that filthy-mouthed, hairy stinking old man') to avoid his advances. (He should have gone out with Maria – he'd have been dead in a day.) Now all that rage had passed, all was emptiness with the wheeling sea birds, the wash of the hissing seas.

*Bombardier Milligan, a moment before looking the other way*

*Me telling Bornheim where my hand has gone.*

*Last shot of Capri before we head for home*

We returned as the evening purple cascaded down on the Sorrentine peninsula.

The ferry is cloyed with chattering screaming Neapolitans and flies. At the stern a row breaks out. I can only see the pictures of a crowd of males hitting one unfortunate individual, some actually hanging over the boat railings to give better purchase for their assault. As in all mobs, anyone can join in the hitting, even though they don't know the reason for it, and even I was tempted. It's the last boat, crowded. We are the only two soldiers on board. I address a seaman: 'Hello sailor,' I say. 'Can you take our picture?' Si. The sailor smiles and points the ancient Kodak. Click! Bornheim and I are immortalized.

The cool evening air and the last warmth of the sun touched our skin. We stood at the rails watching Capri sink into the oncoming crepuscular night; in ancient times the Pharos on Capri would have been igniting its faggot fires to warn ships bearing grain from Africa of its rocky prominence. Bornheim and I were taking on glasses of grappa to light our own faggot fires, and warn those self-same ships against our own rocky prominences. Arriving back at the billets and settling back into the ways of soldiery was difficult. After lights out, we reminisced in our khaki cots. 'It didn't really happen, did it?' he said.


## Nearly!

These were the days when we should have been lotus-eating but the NAAFI didn't stock them. Life was a series of paid gigs. The Bill Hall Trio, with Bornheim on piano and George Puttock on Drums, plays for dances in, around, and sometimes under Naples. Every band in those days had to have an MC. Ours won his at El Alamein. He was Sergeant Bob Hope, yes, *Bob Hope*. What a letdown when he showed up.

'You're not Bob Hope?'

'Oh yes I am.'

'You don't look like Bob Hope.'

'Well, I bloody well am Bob Hope.'

'Not the Bob Hope.'

'No – a Bob Hope.'

We finally got him to use 'Dick' Hope. Dick or Bob, he nearly did for us.

We are in a van returning from a successful gig at the Royal Palace at Caserta, a dead straight road that leads to Naples. There are no lights. Bill Hall is counting and recounting his money, hoping to make it more. He's turning it over for the tenth time.

'You keeping it aired,' says Mulgrew who's got his in a sealed Scottish death grip in his right hand.

Bornheim's lighter illuminates his face; he tries to set fire to Hall's money.

'Wot you bloody doin?' says Hall, beating out the flames.

I'm looking through the windscreen from my bench seat; ahead are two lone sets of car lights; I can tell by their excessive brightness they're American. They are approaching at speed. I have a nasty feeling. The lights are swaying. In no time the car is on us. It veers across to our side. The idiot Dick Hope is rooted to the wheel. I lunge over his shoulder and wrench the steering wheel to the left. As I do so, the uncoming vehicle hits us, there's a screech of metal, it rips the whole of our undercarriage out, our four wheels are hulled from under us and our bodywork crashes to the road. We skid along on the chassis, the road coming up through the floor. We grind to a halt.

'Everyone alright?' shouts Bornheim.

'99, 100,' says Hall, counting his money.

We kick open the rear door and scramble out. The first thing is the unending blare of a motor horn coming from the other vehicle, a banshee sound. It's an American Pontiac staff car, nose deep in a ten-foot ditch. In the dark we slither down. The driver is impaled on the steering column shorting the horn. His eyes have been jettisoned on his cheeks. Dead. We unstick him. In the rear are a colonel and wife/lady/screw. She was unconscious and saying 'O! O! O!' A lot of help – didn't she know any other letters? I drag her out; she's mumbling 'Are you OK, honey?' I said yes, I was honey. Her top half is naked, her dress hanging down from the waist. The colonel is unconscious, his trousers are around his ankles. What I wouldn't have given for a hot line to the *News of the World*! I drag her up the bank. The other three pull the colonel out.

'I think the driver's dead,' says Bill Hall – it must be a second opinion. On the road I help the bird get her boobs back into her dress, give them a squeeze and ask would she like a quickie. The colonel is gaining consciousness and saying 'Darling, you were wonderful' to Bill Hall, who agrees with him. An American Police Patrol jeep screeches to a halt. They leave one policeman and the other speeds off for help – he will 'alert the British Military Police'. In no time the whole mess is cleaned up, the ambulance whisks off the colonel, the lady and the dead driver. A giant crane lifts the wreck away and whoosh! all gone. All that's left are the six British idiots, alone in the dark with the top half of a van. 'Let's play look for the wheels,' says George Puttock.

We are waiting for the 'Alert British Police' – one hour, two hours, three hours – shall we start walking? No, we *should* have started walking hours ago. It's gone four o'clock. Queen Victoria, Abraham Lincoln, Prince Albert had also gone, everyone had gone but us. As morning in a bowl of light was putting the stars to flight, a fifteen-cwt truck with two Military Police arrives, followed by an ambulance. My first words were: 'Where the fuck have you been?' A tall red cap cautions me. 'Now, now Corporal,' he warned, 'that kind of language won't get us anywhere.' Oh, would he like it in fucking French then? He was not endeared to me.

'Where are the injured?' he said.

We *are* the fucking injured, I said, but we're all better now.

'We were told that your driver was dead.'

Oh? We didn't know that, otherwise we would never have let him drive.

Enough is enough. We get into the fifteen-cwt and as the sun was rising, drive down the Royal road to Naples.

'Two hundred, three hundred,' Bill Hall is recounting his

money. Another foot and that car would have killed us. 'Three hundred and twenty . . .'

## Nice Surprisey-Poo

'You are very lucky fellows,' says Reg O'List, who is now not singing 'Begin the Beguine'. Why are we lucky fellows? We have been chosen to appear on the bill of the Finale of the Festival of Arts. This turns out to be nothing more nor less than a Military 'Opportunity Knocks' and, after all the contestants have done, while the summing up is going on, there is to be entertainment by the 'professionals'. Any extra money? No. Sod. O K, the Pros are Stan Bradbury, a song-plugger from the U K, the Polish Ballet, ourselves and . . . HELLLLLPPPPPP Gracie Fields and her singing! It's too late now, we've said yes and they've aired the beds.

'You'll only be there for forty-eight hours,' said Lieutenant O'List. That would be long enough for me to carry out my solemn promise to Maria Marini that I would come back and marry her from the waist down.

'Gracie Fields,' said Bill Hall, like he's announcing the Doppelgänger.

'Don't worry,' says Reg O'List, 'I've put you on before her, so if you hurry up you can be out in the street before she starts singing. I'll try and keep the theatre doors shut so that the sound doesn't get out.'

Secombe, he's coming too, it's about time he came too. Is he going to fill the stage with soap? No. 'I'm on the spotlights,' he says, through his chattering, screaming and farting. Secombe on the spotlights?? That's like putting a man with epilepsy on a tightrope. Secombe can't keep still, he can't concentrate on anything except screaming, shaving and farting. We'll see. 'I've been specially chosen to put the spotlight on Gracie Fields in "Red Sails in the Sunset",' he says, like the Captain of the *Titanic*.

Yet again, the charabanc takes the chosen to the Holy City. This time it's just the Trio, Secombe, and a few spare wanks who will do 'odd jobs back stage'. I have no idea what odd jobs back stage are. Massaging curtains back to life? Mud-wrestling with electricians?

It's the old Albergo Universo, and our lesbian javelin-throwing manager with her fifty-six-inch chest. Can we visit her for a drink after the show? Yes. Have we any free seats? Yes, how many does she want? Seventy-three. She settles for six.

Friday March 1st. We sit in the stalls, watching the amateurs rehearsing for the finals. They are being 'produced' by Major Murray Leslie, Royal Army Service Corps, an ideal corps to produce theatricals. A short dark singer is going through 'Just a song at twilight'. We all know the joke about the short man who looks as though he's been hit by a lift: well, this is the bloke, he's been hit by one from above and another one coming up underneath. He has a good voice, but looks like a semi-straightened-out Quasimodo, and worse, he has ape-like arms. Major Leslie suggests that when the song reaches the climax he raises his arms gradually; they look like two anti-aircraft guns being raised to fire. But there you are. He finishes his song with arms raised. Major Leslie RASC waits a while and says, 'No, no, don't *keep* them up there.'

A woeful series of acts follows. The blond guardsman who recited Wordsworth's 'Daffodils'. For this Major Leslie also suggested the use of the arms, but this time they were raised alternately on 'certain words'.

> I wandered lonely as a cloud (*right arm up*)
> That floats on high o'er vales and hills (*left arm up*)
> When all at once I saw a crowd (*right leg up?*)

and so on. Comes the night, and the hopefuls go through their paces. They get what we would call sympathetic applause, i.e. bugger all. We stand in the wings watching, and keeping an eye out for ''Ow do lads, ee bai gum.' The interval, and the judging goes on. Stan Bradbury 'entertains' at the piano. Why I don't know. A very amiable man, well-loved in the music profession, but an entertainer, no. All the while he played, the audience thought he was the warm-up pianist for a forthcoming singer who never materialized. Now, a last-minute change! The Polish Ballet are playing up and are to go on *before* us; the girls are beautiful, the boys more so; it's a stunning dance company with the full orchestra conducted by Raymond Agoult.

'And now,' it's the announcer Philip Slessor announcing an announcement, 'from the Central Pool of Artists, the Bill Hall . . .'

Before he could get the words out there was a roar from the crowd. We can do no wrong, a smash hit again. The encores keep Gracie Fields trapped in the wings. We take five curtain calls, and then the orchestra plays 'Sally'. On come Gracie, and by the great wave of applause one realizes that none of them have ever heard her Royal Palace NAAFI Naples singing sessions. But disaster lurks for poor Gracie: Gunner Secombe is now poised on the spotlight. He has been told to put the Red Jelly in for when she sings 'Red Sails in the Sunset'. Secombe is myopic: he walks into walls, over cliffs and under streamrollers and in recent years crashed into walls in horse-drawn coaches. In the dark he juggles with the jellies; Miss Fields goes rapturously into 'Red Sails' only to turn green.

'You're going mouldy, Gracie,' shouts a wag. The audience dissolves into tears. Gracie handles it well.

'Sum wun up there don't like me,' she says. Secombe realizes the error and soon Miss Fields is a bright purple, yellow and then orange. Finally someone brings him down with a rugby tackle and before he can do any more damage, he's carried out screaming, shaving and farting.

ARMY WELFARE SERVICES

PRESENT

THE

# C M F

# ARTS FESTIVAL

## ROME 1946

●

FESTIVAL DIRECTOR: Major R. Murray Leslie Rasc
*(O. C. Central Pool of Artistes)*

FESTIVAL CO-ORDINATOR: Capt. Michael Wide, RA

PUBLICITY DIRECTOR: Lieut. C. T. Higgins, RA

THE

CMF ARTS FESTIVAL

PRESENTS

THE

# FESTIVAL FINALE

*Friday. 1 Mar. 1946*

PROGRAMME

1. 'OVERTURE - FESTIVAL VARIETY ORCHESTRA (*Directed by Raymond Agoult CPA*

2. THE CENTRAL POOL OF ARTISTES

PRESENTS

## " WHY THE BELLS OF ST. JOHN'S RANG "

by

Pte ARTHUR WEST, 2nd Bn Mon. Regt.

THE CAST

| | |
|---|---|
| Andreas, the sexton | Edgar Criddle (Tpr) |
| Agnes, his wife | Jacqueline Martig (Ensa) |
| Father John Moser, parson of the neighbouring community | Harry Shacklock L/Cpl |
| George Herman, the Burgomaster | Bernard Collins (LAC) |
| Franz Spirbel | Kenneth Laird (Fus) |
| Peter | Edward Cope (Cpl) |
| Lena | Clemency Davis (Ensa) |
| Father Mathias Meyerhofer, parson of St. John's | John Bailey (Lieut) |

The play produced by Lieut Jordan Lawrence RA
Set designed and painted by Sgt Paul Drago, Cpl John Kimble and Pte Bob Seywood
Set built by Sgt. S. Johnson and Gdsmn G. Swan
Costumes by Sgt Paul Cheese

3. VARIETY OVERTURE - Festival Variety Orchestra
Directed by Raymond Agoult CPA

4. DANCE BAND of the 78th Division (*Competitor in Class B 10*(b))
5. Sigmn. K. McGARRY (*Competitor in Class B 11*(c))
6. Spr C. H. WADE (*Competitor in Class B 11*(a) ii)
7. **STAN BRADBURY** and a Piano
8. Sigmn L. A. RICHARDSON (*Competitor in Class B 11*(c))
9. LACW S. J. MUMSLOW (*Competitor in Class B 11*(a) ii)
10. Pte P. MATTHEWS (*Competitor in Class B 11*(c))
11. **THE BILL HALL TRIO** (Central Pool of Artistes)
12. **POLISH BALLET** - HUNGARIAN RHAPSODY
    *Ballet arranged by K. Ostrowski*
    *Music arranged by Lieut. H Wars*
13. **GRACIE FIELDS**
14. PRESENTATION OF PRIZES

*The King*

*Judges :* MR. A. C. ASTOR, Lt. Col. PHILIP SLESSOR
(*Chief Broadcasting officer C.M.F.*)
MR. STAN BRADBURY and MR. RAY SONIN

COMPETITORS CLASSIFICATIONS
Class B (*Plays and Performers*)
10. (a) UNIT DANCE BANDS.

(b) FORMATION DANCE BANDS

11. (a) iii. LIGHT SINGERS suitable for
Variety or Revue

(iii) DANCE BAND SINGERS

11. (c) SINGLE OR DOUBLE Act
for Variety or Revue

## PRODUCED BY MAJOR R. MURRAY LESLIE (O. C. Central Pool of Artistes)

MUSICAL DIRECTOR - Raymond Agoult CPA
STAGE MANAGER - Sgt. C. Sinkinson Ensa

ASSISTANT PRODUCER - Lieut. R. Priest CPA
HOUSE MANAGER - Capt. R. Orgelist CPA

264

During our act, we have been spotted by an impresario in the Judges' Box who sends us a note promising untold riches in the future.

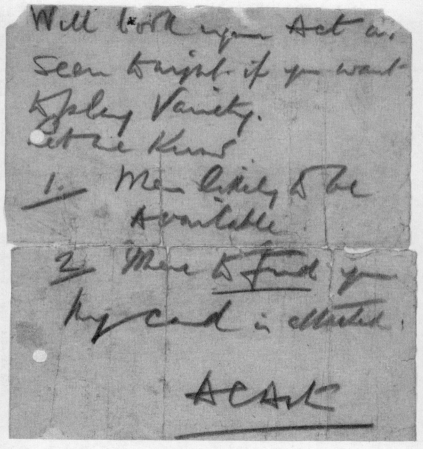

*The note that promised us work in England (original in the British Museum)*

After the show we are all presented to Miss Fields.
''Ow do lads,' she says. 'Ee, I could do with a nice cup o'

tea.' She says she 'looved our act and would we like a nice cup o' tea?'

Captain Reg O'List wants us to have dinner with him again. He treats us to a horse-drawn – 'Mean bugger won't pay for a taxi,' says Hall – again it's spaghetti and wine, and again he will sing 'Begin the Beguine'. I can see by the look in Bill Hall's eyes he fears Reg O'List could become the male Gracie Fields. As the evening goes on, he does, Hall is leaving. 'We got to leave for Naples at nine, Reg.' Too late – Reg O'List has already become Gracie Fields and is singing 'Begin the Beguine'.

# ISCHIA

# Ischia

March 1946. Our cleaning ladies consisted of pretty young Italian things, all on the lookout for potential husbands to take them to Inghilterra. Bornheim and I are pursued by two Marias. (All cleaners in twos are called Marias in Italy.) My Maria I used for laundry, sock repairs and groping.

We decided to take the girls to Ischia as a repayment for squeezing them. When we told them, they shrieked with excitement. No, they'd never been out of Napoli, was there somewhere else? They'd certainly never been to Ischia.

On the Sunday, they turned up carrying raffia baskets full of home-cooked Neapolitan goodies. The ferry was crammed, the noise of their chattering drowning out the engines. Forty minutes and we are there; I try my luck and take us to the Colonel Startling Grope Villa of yore.

Yes, the manservant remembers me of yore – Can we use the private beach? Er – yes. The 'yes' is good, the 'er' is worrying. We disport ourselves and are soon immersed in the sparkling waters. The girls are delirious. Maria I, who is mine, I had only seen in her scruffy working clothes, but now, in her black one-piece bathing costume she is very very dishy and ready to be squongled, and it can't be long now. The girls open the 'hamper'. In half an hour we put on a stone and sink like one. Oh, Neapolitan cooking! We must see the Grotto Azura, says a plying prying boatman. We argue the price and then he rows us to the enchanted hole in the cliff. We enter with our heads ducked and lo, a wonderous luminescent cavern, flickering with diaphanous sunshine on the cavern wall; by a trick of the light we appear to be floating on air. I dive over the side and give an underwater cabaret, in which I look as if I am suspended in air under the boat. It's all wondrous, the girls squeal with delight that echoes round the cavern. Out again into the white sunlight and back to the beach. On dark winter nights I recall that day – the clock should have stopped there. Our 'yes' has run out and the 'er' I was worried about is operating. Er – would we leave now as the owner is returning from Naples where he has been selling packets of sawdust.

We caught the last ferry as twilight fell across the Bay of Naples; pimples of light are starting to appear on the shore. A thousand shouts as we draw to the quay, brown hands grasp the ropes and affix them to rusting bollards. We hire an ancient Fiat taxi that looks like a grave on wheels. It chugs and rattles its way up the slopes of the Vomero. 'Qui, qui, ferma qui,' shout the girls. In the dark there's a brief kissing. We are waving the girls goodbye, when Kerash!! from nowhere a drunk appears and punches through the taxi window.

'Attenzione,' shouts the driver. 'Coltello.' (Look out he's got a knife.) We leap out and set off hot foot. He is shouting something in Italian that sounds like 'My mother keeps legless goats' that can't be right. Why are *we* running away from a man whose mother keeps legless goats? Cowards all! I suddenly stop, turn, thrust my hand inside my battledress pocket and whip out an imaginary pistol.

'Attenzione!' I shout. 'Pistole!' He stops in his tracks and runs away. He could have sung 'Lae thar piss tub dawn bab' but didn't. Very good Milligan. The day ended with a pointed finger. It wasn't the end of a perfect day, but it was an end. 'Who the fuck was he?' said Bornheim, much much further down the hill.

## Civilain Status

The Central Pool of Artists is changed to The Combined Services Entertainment. Why? I suppose it's the result of a 'meeting'. In its wake we, the Bill Hall Trio, are being offered officer status and wages if, when we are demobbed, we sign with the CSE for six months. Hedonists, we all say yes. Officer status? Cor Blimey! All the bloody months in the line and you become Lance-Bombardier. Play the guitar in perfect safety, you become an officer. If I learned the banjo and the tuba I could become a Field-Marshal!

I wrote home and told my delighted parents. Mother proudly informed the neighbours that her son was a 'Banjo-playing Officer'.

COPY OF LETTER ASKING US TO STAY ON SIX MONTH CONTRACT

SUBJECT:- Civilian Employment with C.S.E.

Directorate of Army Welfare Services,

G.H.Q.          C.M.F.

WEL/5193/W2.

18 June 46.

Bdr T.A.Milligan,
Combined Services Entertainment,
Directorate of Army Welfare Services,
G.H.Q.      C.M.F.
_____

1.          It is hereby confirmed that you will accept Local
Release from the Army.

2.          As soon as you are released, it is agreed you will be
employed as an Artist with Combined Services Entertainment,
Directorate of Army Welfare Services, G.H.Q. C.M.F. at a Salary
of £10 per week, plus inclusive Accommodation and Rations and
in accordance with regulations to be laid down for Combined
Services Entertainment.

3.          On your release date you will sign a War Office
contract covering employment with C.S.E. for a period of 6 months.

4.          At the termination of your contract Combined
Services Entertainment will be responsible for arranging your
return to the U.K.

Colonel.

Director of Army Welfare Services.

DKS/JLB.

The signature looks like 'Waolb Petal'. I didn't know we had one. Now, upgrading to officer status caused problems – though still not due for demob till August, we jumped the gun and donned civvies – officers' peaked caps, with green and gold shoulder flash CSE. It was a culture shock for the Officers' Club in Naples when Gunner Bill Hall entered its portals.

''ere! where you goin'?' said the door sergeant, to someone who looked like a dustman.

'I am going in,' said Hall. 'Where *you* goin'?'

The sergeant looked at the thin scruffy apparition in crumpled khaki drill with a fall of cigarette ash on the shirt front. 'This club is for officers,' he said, pointing to the door.

'I am a bleedin' orficer,' said Hall, pointing to himself.

The sergeant demands identification. I watched his face gradually crumple as he read the authorization slip. He gave a sob and walked away. The barman treats Hall like a leper and moves the fly papers nearer.

In his wake, the new-found Officer Hall left a series of broken club secretaries. One offered to sell him a suit, another resigned. Several asked Hall for medical certificates. Mulgrew and his evil sense of humour relished the confrontations. He told how on one occasion at an Officers' Bar, on the approach of Hall, they put newspapers down. He was popularly known in the Officers' Clubs as 'Oh Christ, here he comes', or 'Thank Christ, there he goes'.

### Barbary Coast

Rumours of another show are in the offing. Raymond Ágoult and his wife asked me how would I like to 'write a musical'. I said 'sitting down'. The theme was to be Anne Bonney, the lady pirate, and her lover Calico Jack.

I remember the opening chorus. Lyrics –

> There'll be ten thousand dollars
> For anyone who collars
> Calico Jack.
> CHORUS: Calico Jack!

Again it was too ambitious financially. 'God, Milligan, we'd have to sell the Navy to pay for it,' said Captain O'List.

There's an alternative – it's to be called *Barbary Coast*, a series of variety acts done in an 1880s Bowery Bar setting. The MC is Jimmy Molloy, a forty-year-old Crash Bang Wallop insult-type comic. Jimmy is overweight and over here. The Bill Hall Trio will perform 'as directed', so we wait, directionless, while the wheels of power turn.

Meantime, I must prepare for my civilian status. I must buy clothes to adorn my civilian body and shoes for my civilian feet. Drawing out my savings, I course the Via Roma; for the life of me I could not understand how the Italians could produce such luxurious clothes. There's a wealth of real silk, pure wool, pure cotton garments. I chose a dark

*Me in civvies standing against the statue of Goethe in Rome*

blue corduroy jacket and a lighter pair of trousers, a black and white check sporting jacket with 'British' flannels, three white silk shirts and a blue satin tie, a white polo-neck sweater, all of which would hide my post-war back-up army underwear. One thing I never bought – shoes. I had a pair of huge 'sensible' brown brogues that made my feet look five times the size, shaped like marrows, apparently inflated and about to burst.

'Wot yer want ter buy all that crap for?' says Bill Hall. 'You'll only draw attention to yourself.' I understood him not.

## The Voodoo Moon Club

We would use the rehearsal room, yes! A dance! ORs only! Bornheim, George Puttock and myself took it upon ourselves to turn the room into a London night club. We begged, borrowed, stolen, bribed. I wanted it to look like a giant aquarium. I blacked out windows, filled the space with underwater features, rocks, etc., all from the scenery department, put low-key lighting in, then covered the whole with a large piece of aquamarine perspex. We stapled plain white paper to the scruffy table-tops, hung velvet drapes all round the walls, put green red and blue bulbs into the lights, got the chippies to make music stands with lighting cut-outs with the words VOODOO MOON, that went – like Hollywood marriages – on-off.

Food; our hermetically sealed food flasks we topped with spaghetti bought locally, bottles of local red plonk. Where to serve the food from? Of course! the nearest room – the lavatory opposite. We set up a serving hatch and a masking curtain. From the local ENSA show we try to get Hy Hazell, a strapping in-favour-at-the-time cabaret singer. To wait on table we had massed Marias. Word got around and officers asked if they could come. Yes. 'Make the bastards pay,' said Bill Hall. So we 'Made the Bastards Pay'.

Puttock wants to know. 'Why has it got to be an Aquarium?' What does he think it ought to be? He doesn't know.

*The Bill Hall Quintet in the Voodoo Moon Club*

Well, if you like we can get it done up as an 'I don't know club', and he can stand at the bloody door and when people say what's going on here, he can say 'I don't know.'

I trap my Maria while she is bending down and she is well pleased. Do you still love me Maria? Oh si, si, si, sempre, sempre. Good. Can she and her clutch of Marias act as waitresses on the night? No money, but they'll get danced, groped and allowed to walk home free of charge. Will I marry her and take her to Inghilterra? Of course, yes, si si. The Great Zoll, the master of magic electricity and twit, 'can he help serve the spaghetti from the Karzi?' We need a touch of magic, yes, can he dress up as a sultan for it? Of course, the Spaghetti Sultan, yes, we'll give him that billing. The scenic artist knocks up a sign to go over the Karzi: SPAGHETTI NOW BEING SERVED BY THE GREAT ZOLL, 200 LIRE. I phone the ENSA hotel. Can I speak with Miss Hy Hazell? Un momento. Several un momentos later she speaks. Can she do a cabaret for us? Yes, is there transport? Yes, trams stop at the bottom of the road. Can she bring friends? Yes. How many? Twenty-seven! Sorry, that's too many. OK, then do the bloody cabaret yourself. Of course she can bring twenty-seven.

'We don't want to play orl bloody evening,' says Hall, who has a bint coming. Len Singleton, pianist, comes to the rescue. Not to worry, he will pick up a scratch combination. Name? Oh anything, how about 'Singleton's Black and Whites'?

Perfect, the entire band turns out to be white. The Karzis do niff a little, can we lay it to rest? OK, can the massed Marias wash it with phenyl? Si, si, if I'll marry her and take her to England. Si, si, yes yes, and a quick squeeze of them both.

The Duty Officer Lieutenant Higgins is asking questions. 'What's going on?'

I explain that it's a fine thing we are doing in our spare time to raise the morale of the troops and etc etc etc, and will he go away. Why have we blacked out the windows, the air-raids have stopped. We know sir, but you never know. Have we got permission? Yes. Who from? We don't know yet, but rest assured it will be somebody.

*At the Voodoo Moon Club, the Riding High Band sit in.* 1st Trumpet: *Dave Douglas;* 2nd Trumpet: *Roy Duce;* Alto: *Billy Wells;* Piano: *Dennis Evans;* Bass: *J. Mulgrew (anything for extra money!), and the singer, Norman Lee*

Comes the night, it was a bomb-out success. Finished at 0400! Bornheim, Puttock and I made 10,000 lire each and as many enemies.


## A Day Out

Seven of us hired a taxi and went swimming at Bagnoli. The beach was in the ancient Campi Flegrei, one time watering place of the Roman rich. A pumice-coloured beach, a few run-down bathing huts, the doors swung on rusty hinges, the cabins now used by beach whores for 'quickies'; a dying Italian hires out worn umbrellas. Several fishing craft bob in the morning calm sea. A rip-roaring day with skylarking in and out of the sea. We hire a row boat and soon we are going in all directions; we round the headland of the Isle of Nisidia and turn into a horseshoe bay. We discover caves! Wow, it's an omni-directional day; totally mindless, we strip off and dive off the jagged lava rocks.

Bang, bang! Bullets are flying over our heads.

'It's World War Three and they've started without us,' I shouted, ducking for cover. From down the craggy hillside come armed carabinieri. They are shouting. We take to the oars and row like mad in all directions; we would have moved faster if we had just drifted. I am shouting 'Ferma! Sono Inglese.'

A good-looking Italian captain, speaking like George Sanders with garlic, asks what we are doing. What a sight we make, three of us naked save shirts, two totally naked, one naked with socks on, me in a pair of groin-crippling underpants pretending I am Tarzan in my brown boiled boots.

'We are swimming,' I say, forgetting I am standing on land.

'This is a prohibited area,' he says.

I tell him *we* are prohibited people, but he doesn't understand.

'This is a top security island,' he says, 'where war criminals

*Two years in the front line – Army food!*

top: *At end of day to a trattoria for dinner*
centre: *Spike after a good dinner*
left: *The waiter who served us*

*Swimming starkers*

are being held.' I ask him what part are they being held by, but he still doesn't understand and waves his Beretta pistol. I wave back, he is getting angry, we must leave.

In total disarray we clamber into our craft. Have you read *Three Men in a Boat*? – well, multiply that by seven. Everyone rowed furiously in a different direction, the boat was coming apart. As the Italians were threatening and shooing us away, the Captain said something to his men and they all burst out laughing. As they were laughing in Italian we couldn't understand it. I looked at my motley crew and realized how lucky Captain Bligh had been.

My God! A squall blows up! Soon we are bailing for our *lives*! A boatman from the shore takes us in tow, we are very grateful until he asks for two hundred lire. We argue, he explains that we would never have made it back on our own. 'Fuck off,' says Barlow to a man who has just saved our lives. What a day!

'Dear Mother, Today we went swimming and were nearly shot at by Italians and drowned, wish you were here.'

We jump aboard one of the shuttle passion waggons throbbing on the beach, filled with spent soldiers. Why are we waiting? 'My mate's having a shag in that hut.' He points to a fragile beach hut shaking backwards and forwards under the assault from within, then there's a pause. ''ees 'avin a rest,' says the soldier, the hut starts to vibrate again, the door opens and out comes a weed of a soldier who gets a desultory cheer from his mates, a portly tart hoisting up her bathing costume frames in the doorway, waving him goodbye with the money.

'Orl finished shaggin'?' cries the driver, cries of yes, and we lollop forward over the sand on to the road and away. As we sped down the coast road I was stricken with the divine view and had a shot at taking a photograph. It doesn't exactly do justice to the scene, but it's evidence to say that I'm not making this all up.

June 17th 1946. *Barbary Coast* opened at the Bellini Theatre: a packed house, with soldiers queuing all day. Again the Bill Hall Trio, with a lot more gags in the act,

*Photo of Naples Bay – to prove it was there*

steal the show; a corps de ballet from Rome did next best –
all top-class dancers and only in this show because Rome
Opera House is temporarily closed.

Great write-ups the next day! Then the icing on the cake:
we are to tour, but this time we are to include Venice and
Vienna! Someone should have told us, 'Man, these are the
best days of your life, eat them slowly.'

Sunday morning, all bustle and packing kit on to the
charabanc, Gunner Hall as usual is missing.

'She must be late paying him,' says Bornheim. All set, we
pile on to the CSE charabanc with Umberto the fat Iti
driver pinning Holy Pictures on the dashboard to ward off
the devil, accidents, Protestants and the husband of the
woman he is knocking off.

It's a sparkling day, the sun streaming through the holes
in Bornheim's underwear. 'What's this Venice like?' he says.
I tell him when you step out the front door you go splash!
People don't take dogs for a walk, they take fish. Wasn't the

city resting on piles? Yes, it was agony for the people underneath.

Lieutenant Priest boards the charabanc. 'Answer your names,' he says. 'Bornheim G.' 'Sah,' we all shout. 'Mulgrew J?' 'Sah' we all answer. He tears up the list in mock defeat; the charabanc and its precious cargo of piss artists proceeds forth. We inch thru the unforgettable fish market off the Piazza Capuana, displaying everything from water-fleas to tuna on the barrows. The mongers douse their catches with water. 'Fools,' says Bornheim. 'They'll never revive them.' The church bells are anointing the air, each peal sending flocks of pigeons airborne on nervous wings. Through the machicolated crowds we edge, finally arriving at the peeling front of the Albergo Rabacino, which roughly translated means Rabies. Ronnie Priest flies into its front portals. He's annoyed – the Italian ballerinas from our cast are not ready. 'They had to go to holy bloody mass,' he says. We all get out and stretch our legs and are immediately beset with vendors. I am casting my eye on a tray of watches that gleam gold like the riches of Montezuma. They are in fact cheapo watches dipped in gold-plating. I knock the price down from ten million lire to ten thousand. OK, I buy the watch. Of course it doesn't give the date, phases of the moon, high tide in Hawaii, it doesn't light up in the dark, doesn't give electronic peals every half hour, and it doesn't ring like an alarm in the morning. All it does is tell the silly old time.

I paid the vendor and told him the time, I said hello to Mulgrew and told him the time, I called Bornheim over and told him the time and I wrote a letter to my mother telling her the time. Looking at the watch I realize it's time to close this fifth volume of my War Time Trilogy. It was the year I had left the front line and found various Base Depot jobs. I had much to be thankful for and now I knew the time. In Volume Six I will tell the time and the story of my love affair with Maria Antoinette Pontani, the Italian ballerina who in a way changed my life and made me abandon my store of second-hand Army underwear. The time is 11.20 a.m.

# SPIKE MILLIGAN

## MILLIGAN'S MEANING OF LIFE
AN AUTOBIOGRAPHY OF SORTS

Containing never-seen-before letters and photographs, here at last is the full story of Spike Milligan's life – all in his own words

With his lightning-quick wit, unbridled creativity and his ear for the absurd, Milligan revolutionised British comedy, leaving a legacy of influence that stretches from Monty Python's Flying Circus to the work of self-confessed acolytes such as Eddie Izzard and Stephen Fry today.

Throughout his life, Milligan wrote prolifically – scripts, poetry, fiction, as well as several volumes of memoir, in which he took an entirely idiosyncratic approach to the truth. In this ground-breaking work, Norma Farnes, his long-time manager, companion, counsellor and confidante, gathers together the loose threads, reads between the lines and draws on the full breadth of his writing to present his life in his own words: an autobiography – of sorts.

From his childhood in India, through his early career as a jazz musician and sketch-show entertainer, his spells in North Africa and Italy with the Royal Artillery, to that fateful first broadcast of The Goon Show and beyond into the annals of comedy history, this is the autobiography Milligan never wrote.

'Milligan is the Great God to all of us'  John Cleese

'The Godfather of Alternative Comedy'  Eddie Izzard

'My father had a profound influence on me. He was a lunatic.'  Spike Milligan

# SPIKE MILLIGAN

**PUCKOON**

'Spike Milligan's novel bursts at the seams with superb comic characters involved in unbelievably likely troubles on the Irish border' *Observer*

The only full-length novel that Milligan wrote, *Puckoon* is a masterpiece of verbal wit and surreal imagination. It tells of the adventures of Dan Milligan, who has been living off his wits and his pension ('both hopelessly inadequate') since partition, and his haphazard quest for work in the Irish border village of Puckoon in the midst of the troubles.

Loved by generations and considered by many to be one of the funniest novels of its era, it is pure Milligan madness from start to finish.

'Pops with the erratic brilliance of a careless match in a box of fireworks' *Daily Mail*

# SPIKE MILLIGAN

**THE BIBLE ACCORDING TO SPIKE MILLIGAN: THE OLD TESTAMENT**

1. In the beginning God created the Heaven and the Earth.

2. And darkness was upon the face of the deep; this was due to a malfunction at Lots Road Power Station.

3. And God said, Let there be light; and there was light, but Easter Electricity Board said He would have to wait until Thursday to be connected.

4. And God saw the light and it was good; He saw the quarterly bill and it was not good.

There have been many versions of the Old Testament over the centuries but never one quite like this. Here Spike Milligan rewrites in his own inimitable style many of its best-known stories, featuring characters such as King (my brain hurts) Solomon, the great oaf of a giant Goliath and the well-known *Telegraph* crossword clue, Hushai the Archite. One of his best-known and most irreverent works of creation, it will have believers and non-believers alike rolling with laughter and worshipping Milligan's eternal wit.

'Milligan is the Great God to all of us' John Cleese

# SPIKE MILLIGAN

## HIDDEN WORDS: COLLECTED POEMS

Everyone knows and loves Spike Milligan for his amazing comic genius. This collection of his poems, however, reveals other sides to him that we may not have met before.

There is Spike the adoring father who has written some intensely poignant poems for his children, and there is Spike the soldier, mourning the deaths of his comrades during the War. Spike the lover, the family man and the concerned environmentalist also appear in this volume of his poetry, at times touching, sometimes tender, occasionally angry and often extremely funny.

Written over a span of some twenty years, *Hidden Words* contains all of the poems from *Small Dreams of a Scorpion*, *Open Heart University* and *The Mirror Running*, as well as some additional work, and is a brilliantly diverse and surprising collection of poetry.

# He just wanted a decent book to read ...

Not too much to ask, is it? It was in 1935 when Allen Lane, Managing Director of Bodley Head Publishers, stood on a platform at Exeter railway station looking for something good to read on his journey back to London. His choice was limited to popular magazines and poor-quality paperbacks – the same choice faced every day by the vast majority of readers, few of whom could afford hardbacks. Lane's disappointment and subsequent anger at the range of books generally available led him to found a company – and change the world.

*'We believed in the existence in this country of a vast reading public for intelligent books at a low price, and staked everything on it'*
**Sir Allen Lane, 1902–1970, founder of Penguin Books**

The quality paperback had arrived – and not just in bookshops. Lane was adamant that his Penguins should appear in chain stores and tobacconists, and should cost no more than a packet of cigarettes.

Reading habits (and cigarette prices) have changed since 1935, but Penguin still believes in publishing the best books for everybody to enjoy. We still believe that good design costs no more than bad design, and we still believe that quality books published passionately and responsibly make the world a better place.

So wherever you see the little bird – whether it's on a piece of prize-winning literary fiction or a celebrity autobiography, political tour de force or historical masterpiece, a serial-killer thriller, reference book, world classic or a piece of pure escapism – you can bet that it represents the very best that the genre has to offer.

**Whatever you like to read – trust Penguin.**